NICOLÓ ANDREULA   VERA SPROTHEN

FLOW
GENERATION

A SURVIVAL GUIDE FOR OUR UNPREDICTABLE LIVES

Published by Daimonriver Press
61 Macwood Road
Smiths Lake NSW 2428, Australia

Cover design by Stefano Solarino

ISBN 978-0-646-80504-7 (paperback)

All expert and protagonist quotes in this book are taken from interviews conducted exclusively for this book, unless otherwise referenced.

www.flowgenerationbook.com

For Leo and Paula,
because you're never too small to dream big.
—V.S.

For Amelia,
my guardian angel.
—N.A.

Content

Part I

Part II

Part I

How did we end up here?

Why does everything suddenly feel so loose? Not long ago, things had a place. Clouds were in the sky. Telephones were plugged into the wall. And work was something you "went to". We, too, had a clear idea of where we belonged. If someone asked us where we'd see ourselves in three years' time, we weren't shy of answers because our world seemed predictable back then.

Looking into the future felt like playing "Game of Life", this board game where life unfolds on a clear-cut path, with some shortcuts and detours, but ultimately a sequence of regular paydays and boxes to tick. In the game you only need to spin the wheel of fortune, draw the right career card to become a doctor or race car designer, and eventually earn enough money to go on vacation, raise a family and pick your dream home: beach hut or mountain villa, city penthouse or mansion.

Today, everything is all over the place. Our work, our phones, ourselves. The game of life has become messy.

Never before has technological progress spread so rapidly and disrupted so many areas of our lives at once. Digital tools and automation, big data and algorithms are changing how we earn money and spend it, whom we trust, what we learn and where we go on holidays. Today, we open a smartphone app to find love and use a robot to get a job done. If we still have a job. Because secure, permanent, full-time employment is in decline in our fast-paced, data-driven economies and this trend is shaking the foundations on which generations before us have built their life's success.

Unlike our parents, we are left with no clear-cut recipe on how to make it safely to retirement. As our traditional career paths dissolve, we are forced to ask fundamental questions: How will I earn money tomorrow? Does going to uni still get me a job? Shall I farewell the dream of buying a home if my freelance status can't get me a loan? Who will take care of my health and pension? Have I already sold my soul by joining online social networks and customer loyalty programs or can I make money with my personal data?

It's like our lives have turned liquid. We are the "Flow Generation".

***

ADRIÁN. MADRID. SEARCHING FOR A JOB.

Adrián Penalva Soler kicks the fridge door shut and takes a sip of black coffee. There is no more milk and the biscuits are dry. He has to go shopping. And get fresh air before the heat grows unbearable in his apartment that also serves him as a working space.

At night, when the hum of the highway ebbs, Adrián leaves the kitchen window open. But now Madrid's city traffic is thundering again, despite the graffiti-stained noise barrier that cuts through the wasteland behind his place. It was the cheapest he could find. Expensive for what he earns. His friends from back home, a small village in the south of Spain, call his rent outrageous.

Still, it's Madrid, the capital, where an audiovisual content producer like himself can be successful and afford a better life. Adrián moved here in 2014 to get a master's degree and finally find a proper job after a string of casual stints. Something in a film production firm. But his hopes for solid, long-term, well-paying employment never pan out. Spanish companies aren't in hiring mood.

Five years after graduating, with two university degrees and four languages on his resume, Adrián still finds himself in limbo. He jumps back and forth between internships and part-time work, between short-term contracts and joblessness. No role is lasting, and no employer offers more than 700 euros a month.

Eventually, Adrián gives up on the full-time dream and goes freelance, taking film production projects as they come. They keep him afloat. But every so often he faces months like this one, where work goes slow or a client skips an invoice, and Adrián needs to make a tough decision: pay rent or buy groceries. "I'm almost 30 but I still have no economic stability," says Adrián. "I'm staying in Madrid only because my family continues to help me out financially."

ALESSANDRO. CAPE TOWN. LOOKING FOR AN EXIT.

The wind is howling and Alessandro Mazzi feels the pull of the kite in his arms. He is speeding over the lagoon, flying at times as the gusts lift him metres into the air, and when they punch him back down, he hits the water hard, but the board holds. It's strong. As strong as he hoped it would be. As strong as myself, he thinks.

"I'm free to do whatever," he had told himself when he veered off a path that always looked like the right one – until one day it didn't.

He had studied law, moved from Italy to China for an internship, then to Hong Kong, and to Australia, where he joined a large corporate law firm. His parents were proud. But after one of those hellish 70-hour weeks, when his flatmates asked him what he'd rather do, Alessandro's reply came like a bullet: kitesurf instructor.

Idiotic? Only months ago, his dad's construction company had gone bankrupt. And here was Alessandro weighing a safe legal career against a come-as-you-are existence spent kitesurfing. Yet he couldn't let go of the idea. He was looking for an exit from the corporate world. Some Plan B. Maybe he could teach kitesurfing until he worked out how to use his law skills in a different way. And what is security anyway? He always thought of his dad's firm as a rock, and now what? A lifetime's achievement crumbled to pieces.

He remembers his older brother telling him it'd be fine, he'd be fine. His life. His future. It was much needed mental support as he prepared for the unknown.

"Security is an illusion," Alessandro thinks, as he hoists the wet board into the van, the air chilly now in Cape Town. The law firm is far away, and he is free. It feels good and scary at the same time.

LACHLAN. VALENCIA. SHUT OUT OF SCHOOL.

From afar he can see the police cars cordoning off the schoolyard like a crime scene, and Lachlan feels his muscles tense up. As he approaches the gate, the uniformed man doesn't flinch, his hand stretched out like a shield in front of him. "Cerrado! Closed!" the man says, signalling him to move away from the building, where he and the other expat kids are lingering like ship-wrecked sailors.

You don't argue with the Guardia Civil, the Spanish military force charged with police duties. When they enter your classroom and tell you to leave, like they did the day before, you better leave. But he feels it: fight or flight. Just a reflex, but there have been too many of these moments this year – the year when the financial crisis tears down Lachlan's world. He is 16 and four months away from his final exams when his private high school goes out of business.

Born in Dubai to Scottish parents, he's lived in Spain for much of his teenagehood. The country had been doing well. His family had bought a house not far from the sea. Some of their friends own two when the turmoil breaks loose: stock markets in freefall, the world's biggest banks teetering. Lachlan's dad lost his job in the oil industry and the family home is dropping in value by the day. And now the school ...shut down.

Should be doable, Lachlan thinks after the first shock has subsided. Alternative English-speaking schools in his area are out of reach. Too expensive. So he convinces his parents to let him finish his high school certificate in self-study from home. He also insists on becoming a personal trainer instead of pursuing the psychologist career he had always dreamed of. Getting some hands-on work experience seems like a good idea in these uncertain times.

But Lachlan underestimates the emotional toll of the crisis. He watches in disbelief as his mum pawns her Middle Eastern jewellery for cash and it pushes him to work harder. The gym becomes his lifeline. He spends

12-hour days training and learning by heart the Latin names of every muscle in his body. At night, he falls asleep over his textbooks. It's too much. When the letter arrives that he has officially failed his high school exam, it doesn't even come as a surprise.

What do you do when your life gets messed up by something bigger than you? Lachlan has missed the key entry hurdle into formal education. Could he do without? Could he figure out on his own what skills he'd need to make a living?

It's one of those fight-or-flight moments. Lachlan decides to fight.

VERA. SYDNEY. LOOKING FOR A HOME.

Maybe tonight. Maybe after dinner. It's never the right moment, Vera thinks. But after dinner might be good. She will drop the fork, pull the ultrasound image out of the back pocket of her jeans and announce the end of this house share.

She smells the scent of coconut curry wafting from the kitchen down the long narrow corridor that connects the house's living quarters like an artery. The lounge room with the old velvety sofa, mossy green and scuffed, but too comfortable to throw out. The makeshift office room with its surfboard racks and bookshelves. And the three bedrooms with their flywire-screened windows that let the sunlight in, but also the noise and the dirt from the garbage trucks which rumble past every morning to collect binloads of empty beer bottles from the bars and eateries on the other side of the laneway.

Vera is 29 and a freelance journalist, when she finds out she is pregnant. Money comes and goes, depending on the number of articles she manages to sell to overseas newspapers. But even if the fickle currency exchange rate keeps working in her favour, she'd never earn enough to rent a house with a papaya tree in the garden. Not in Sydney's eastern beach suburbs. Land here is scarce and property prices have spiralled out of control, since a resources boom began to suck thousands of foreign workers into the country.

Soon Vera and her boyfriend would have to rely on one income. They both live in the share house, but will likely need to move into one of those stuffy little apartments in the area. Pay a premium for one without smelly carpets and mouldy walls. Or they could do what families normally do: bite the bullet of long commutes and move into the city's outer suburbia, so their kids can grow up playing cricket in the backyard. But then again, what is normal these days, and what is right?

Vera feels uneasy, as she enters the kitchen where her flatmate Isabelle is chopping coriander while Jason, the Canadian, is opening a beer. "Want one?" he asks. Vera shakes her head. "There's something I need to tell you guys," she says, fumbling with the ultrasound image.

And then, when the hullaballoo has finally died down, Vera asks Isabelle if she heard her correctly. "Yes," she repeats. "Isn't it great? We're having a share house baby!"

She firmly believes four flatmates could raise a child in a shared house.

***

The decisions facing Adrián, Alessandro, Lachlan and Vera are symptomatic of our times. These young people thought they were on track until they realised with a shiver that their track had disappeared in a world that is changing faster than our sense of security can keep up with.

Are we ready for an even less foreseeable future?

You may think that you're at the mercy of the elements or the ability of some distant captain to navigate rough waters, but the reality is that you're not. This book will teach you how to survive in these choppy waters. Treat it like a life vest that can give you the confidence to look ahead with optimism.

If you want answers on how to work, learn, live and build your own safety net in this brave new world, go straight to the second part of this book. But try to see the bigger picture first. The more you understand, the better your strategy.

So how the hell did we end up here?

Let's investigate.

No man ever steps in the same river twice,
for he is not the same man
and it is not the same river.
— Heraclitus

Chapter 1

Turbulent times: "It's crazy out there"

Two thousand five hundred years ago, in a small coastal town in Turkey, a bearded man found an eternal truth on the shores of a river. For hours he had been sitting there, lost in thought as he watched the water move and drift and swirl, past the bend and down toward the valley, where the stream emptied into the Aegean Sea. The man sighed. *"Panta rei,"* he thought. *"Everything flows."*

The man's name was Heraclitus, a Greek philosopher famous for his aphorisms. Born in the city of Ephesus, then part of the Persian Empire, he described the nature of the world, and of life itself, as a constant transformation. Everything is in flux, never static or still. "No man ever steps in the same river twice," he stated, "for he is not the same man and it is not the same river".

Heraclitus was a bit of a loner, a melancholic man who enjoyed solitude. Traditional paintings often depict him in dark clothes, wringing his hands over the world. "The weeping philosopher" others called him. He lived in a simple age, when most people farmed the land. Life was hard, knowledge scant and change slow. Yet his wisdom has endured over millennia and in our fast-paced, high-tech economies, his insights are more relevant than ever. They continue to inspire the most eminent philosophers, economists and scientists, for if one thing is dependable in our world, it is constant change.

Our times are VUCA: volatile, uncertain, complex and ambiguous. Originally coined by the US army to describe the global power balance after the collapse of the Soviet Union, this four-letter acronym is now a trendy managerial catch-all for "Hey, it's crazy out there!", according to the *Harvard Business Review*.[1] You will hear it in corporate boardrooms from London to Chicago, where business leaders are under pressure to make million-dollar decisions in a world where the facts of today are the falsehoods of tomorrow, or even of later today.

There's chaos everywhere. Just try to keep up with your Twitter newsfeed for 24 hours. It's impossible. We didn't anticipate Brexit and the election of Donald Trump startled even himself.

We see cybercrime and climate change, meteoric startups, crashing stock markets and collapsing states. There are bitcoins and bubbles, speech recognition systems and self-driving cars, data scandals and privacy breaches and stupid household robots that may be spying on us. Everything is at risk of becoming digital or automated or ready to pop and you may lose all your money, your job, your house and your soul.

What's going on?

Whatever it is, it's messy. Everything seems VUCA, and it fuels our fear of losing control over our lives. A whole bunch of researchers is busy measuring the fear factor in society. There are surveys tracking our fear of economic instability, our fear of pollution and climate change, our fear of terrorism, our fear of missing out and our fear of "being outside the comfort zone".

Every year the World Economic Forum, that prestigious non-profit funded by about a thousand global companies, asks several hundred leading experts and decision-makers how they feel about the future. In January 2018 its Global Risk Perception Survey cautioned that "we are struggling to keep up with the accelerating pace of change" and the "widespread uncertainty, instability and fragility" worldwide.[2] Nearly 60 per cent of respondents expected global risks to increase in the coming year, compared to only 7 per cent who thought they would decline.

Prominent figures like Angel Gurría, Secretary General at the OECD, an organisation representing the world's most developed countries, add to that unsettled feeling. He argues that we are facing "unprecedented unpredictability".[3] But is the unpredictability really *unprecedented*? Is today's world crazier than it was in the past? Have our lives ever been anything but liquid?

Heraclitus saw life as a river that carries us along. But how do we stay afloat when the river flows more swiftly and the safety rafts we once built for ourselves look increasingly frail?

A large body of economic research reveals that the river is indeed flowing faster every year because technological progress is changing our economies at an exponential rate. The impact of new technology is so strong and happens so fast that the institutions and the mindset we've been relying on for decades aren't keeping up. They are crumbling.

The new technology is so varied and unforeseeable, and its effects are so sweeping that the life patterns

11

we've expected for decades are fading away. Rapid advances in automation, artificial intelligence and digital technology are killing industries and threatening our job security. Large companies, pillars of the economy, are disappearing from the top tiers of stock markets more frequently than in the past. Bigger and bigger swings in corporate earnings are making it harder for us to predict the growth of our retirement money. And the rise of social media as our new real-time communication tool means we see and hear about every little crack around us the minute it occurs.

What does all this mean? The river that is our world is moving faster, yes, but that's not all. It's altering in essence, becoming a new kind of river, a flow Heraclitus couldn't have imagined. The nature of change is actually changing. It is becoming more intricate and less comprehensible.

Look closely at today's river. You'll see countless ribbons of current, each one moving with a different speed, size, turbulence, and lifespan. You can ride one, or use your agility and glide along on two or more. But they're all morphing before our eyes, so your ribbon can narrow, turn tumultuous, then slow, and vanish while you're on it. It can grow rough enough to toss you onto another current, perhaps to your surprise. Meanwhile, new currents keep springing up, and it's hard to tell what kind of ride they'll offer and how long they'll exist. And the river keeps widening and widening, far beyond the banks where Heraclitus once sat, beyond the power of the eye to scan.

That's our VUCA world.

How do we stay afloat on that? We can't just drift. If we try to stay in a single lane, it may fling us off or disappear. We have to know how to move from one to another, catch what we can, negotiate the complex and incessant changes, find our way. No wonder we feel lost, left on our own in wild waters with waves surging erratically and no end in sight.

If Heraclitus were still alive, he would probably tell us that our perception is the problem because the river remains a river, whether it is an ordinary stream or a quick-shifting mix of currents. It's still always water. We just need to trust that we can learn how to stay afloat.

The way we look at things can make a difference. A road only leads uphill if you stand at the bottom. If you stand at the top, it slopes down.

Up and down, fast and slow, good and bad – it depends on your perspective, but you're ultimately always describing the same thing, two sides of the same coin. This theory, known by Heraclitus scholars as the "Unity of Opposites", is a cornerstone of modern relativism, and contains good news for anyone facing a difficult situation. Heraclitus is telling us that nothing is ever set in stone, including ourselves.

If we perceive something as a threat, it inevitably also offers an opportunity. And if we feel overwhelmed as the world goes VUCA, we may just as well feel excited because we hold inside us the seeds of opposite traits that we can grow in different moment of our lives.

"As the same thing there exist in us living and dead, waking and sleeping, young and old," Heraclitus said. "From all things one, and from one all things."

What does this mean?

It shows we already have within us what it takes to master the increasingly turbulent flow of our lives. Where there's fear, there must be courage. And where a river has countless strands, it has countless opportunities. We can live as no one has ever lived before, on multiple paths that fulfil our complex natures. So let's take a detailed look at the growing uncertainty that is worrying us as workers, consumers and investors.

Once we understand why the world has accelerated so much, we can figure out what to do about it.

Holding onto the income rollercoaster

We feel more precarious, and it's not just in our heads. Our economies, the companies that sustain them, and the stock markets they move have become more instable. Part of this has to do with the Global Financial Crisis, which wiped out billions of dollars from corporate balance sheets and personal bank accounts worldwide.

The crisis dented the confidence of millions of people. In a recent survey, every second American reported being afraid of "not having enough money for the future".[4] In Europe, more than 60 per cent of people surveyed by the Pew Research Center in 2016 considered "global economic instability" a major threat for their countries. The economic concerns are particularly high in Greece (95%) and Spain (84%), where the wounds of the crisis are still healing.[5]

The worries are real.

It has indeed become more difficult to predict the growth of our retirement money because the share of our savings that sits in a pension fund typically ends up in one way or another in the stock market. There is clear evidence that stock markets are more volatile today than they were in the past.

Yet the rollercoaster up-and-downs in the world of money had already become more pronounced in the years before the Global Financial Crisis. McKinsey research shows that swings in corporate earnings have increased sharply over the past 50 years. For example, had you bought shares of a large North American company in the 1970s, your return would have been 60 per cent more predictable than the return of such a purchase in the new millennium.[6]

The lifespan of companies is more and more just a guess. Firms are under constant pressure to remain relevant in highly competitive markets with rapidly shifting consumer tastes and increasingly vocal shareholders. The result: more fluctuation in the business world. Look at the S&P 500, which comprises the 500 most valuable companies listed on Wall Street. In 1930, the average corporation could expect to stay on this index for 75 years. Today, its life expectancy has fallen to 15 or 25 years, depending on the estimate you look at.[7]

Private investors or rival companies buy some companies, but others merge or simply go bankrupt. And while some tech corporations are now bigger and more powerful than entire nations, their lustre can fade quickly if they fail to innovate. A business that wants to stay on top these days has to move much faster.

Seventeen employers, five careers

As companies more often change direction to harness latest technologies and keep up with their shapeshifting markets, they restructure and reorganise, shut down old divisions and create new roles. We have to adjust. Our careers become more unpredictable and volatile. The old straight, single path is now jagged and multiple.

We have become a generation of job hoppers. For example, a study found that in the late 1970s a typical American twentysomething-year-old (the "baby boomer" generation) lasted four years in one job before switching to a new one. This might sound like an eternity for a twentysomething "millennial" today, who typically holds a job for just one year, according to the same study.[8]

Europeans are also changing employers more frequently. Leaving all demographic trends and other distracting variables aside, the average job tenure in European Union countries shrank by around three months over the decade to 2012, according to a study by EU agency Eurofound.[9]

The trend will likely accelerate in the future. In the US, workers are switching jobs at the fastest rate since the internet boom 17 years ago.[10] In Australia, projections based on current job market data suggest that the average 18-year-old today can expect to work for 17 different employers and change careers five times until retirement.[11]

Why is this so? Let's revisit Heraclitus, who says *it is not the same river* and, importantly, *we are not the same men* (and women).

Studies show that young people today have a different attitude towards work than their parents and grandparents. Many millennials value purpose, flexibility, autonomy and independence more than financial stability. You could say they are generally more comfortable with an unpredictable working life.

Still, technology is probably the fundamental driving force behind our accelerated working lives. The job market's higher speed is largely driven by a gear shift in its engine. In other words, swift, multi-faceted technological progress in a globalised world is making our careers more volatile as companies change in response to it.

Employers can now use an array of technologies to do work faster and more effectively. There is automation and artificial intelligence (AI), big data technology and blockchain networks, digital platforms and remote working software, sensor-led systems, crowd solutions and cloud services.

These innovations have had an increasingly indiscriminate impact. They affect everyone – low-skilled factory labourers as well as high-skilled professionals and creatives.

In 2016, the *Washington Post* began to "employ" robots to produce automated news briefs about sports and politics.[12] Surgical robots are becoming a common sight in operating theatres. And experts believe it is only a matter of time until an AI-composed song becomes a hit on the charts.[13]

From the invention of the steam engine to the jet plane, technology has always pushed humankind to a new level. Still, the latest wave of technological progress, the Digital Revolution, is unlike anything we've seen before because of its pace, its pervasiveness and the way it overwhelms our perception. And though we sense each of them, few of us grasp their full extent.

Why do we underestimate its pace?

Every few months, electronics stores advertise new products: larger smartphones, thinner laptops, and sensor-controlled devices that connect with the internet and each other. Robots are rapidly entering our homes and our workplaces. Not a week goes by without the prompt for a software update or app download.

The speed with which new digital technology is taking over our lives doesn't just *feel* overwhelming. It actually *is*. It is bursting the seams of our capacity to adapt because our learning curves are linear and technology improves exponentially, writes Pulitzer Prize winner Thomas Friedman in *Thank You For Being Late*.

When Friedman and other prominent thinkers describe the explosive growth of digital innovation, they
typically refer to a simple yet far-reaching observation
made by an American electronics engineer named
Gordon Moore in the 1960s. Moore, co-founder of microchip producer Intel, was one of the pioneers of the
modern IT industry. He realised early on how radically
computers would alter our way of living.

At the time, computers were still heavy machines
with bulky monitors and server towers that barely fit
beneath a desk. However, Moore had noticed how
quickly circuit boards – those green rectangular plastic
sheets full of electronic nodes and plugs and wires that
powered early computers – were becoming crowded. In
fact, Moore saw that the number of transistors per
square inch was roughly doubling every year.

The discovery led him to make an extraordinary prediction. In the future, he said, computers would become
twice as powerful every year. While Moore later lowered
the rate of change, conceding that computer power
would likely double only every 18 to 24 months, its
essence remains valid even today.

Known as "Moore's Law", this rule of thumb shows
that digital technological advances are anything but
gradual. They occur at increasingly rapid speed.

Of course, breakthrough innovations occur in every
discipline and industry. Farmers switched from hand
ploughs to tractors, and the land transport industry
moved from horse carriages to cars. But the pace of the
Digital Revolution is unique. Suppose the automobile
industry had evolved as rapidly as the microchip
industry under Moore's Law. A Volkswagen Beetle built
in 1971 would today resemble a rocket, able to accelerate
to 480,000 kilometres per hour and consuming about one

litre of petrol per over 800,000 kilometres, writes Friedman. What's more, the cost of developing such a vehicle would be just 4 cents.[14]

Do you see how big Moore's Law is?

The Digital Revolution is unique and exciting, but Moore's Law makes it unsettling because of two features. First, it grows exponentially: it's a technological wave that started as a ripple, but is swelling very fast. Second, it continues to surge with no peak in sight, more than 50 years after it started.

Imagine you had grown up near a river, placid and calm. On your 25th birthday, someone tells you that the slightest ripple on the river's water surface would from now on double in size every year.

Initially, you might not care. It's a very smooth river and the ripples are just one millimetre high – about the width of a plastic ID card – so as you sunbathe floating on your back you don't even notice them. After one year they are two millimetres high, still unnoticeable, and after four years they are 16 millimetres or 1.6 centimetres high. You could now detect them – barely.

After 10 years, when you turn 35, the tiny ripple has become a one-metre wave you can't possibly ignore. Still, you learnt how to swim a long time ago. You can duck underwater and wait for the waves to pass. Or just go with the flow and enjoy the ride.

But on your 40th birthday the swell in front of you is 32 metres high, taller than an eight-storey building and almost as high as the worst waves off Cape Horn. You manage – just. You've built yourself a very sturdy boat and you know how to handle the onslaught, but when you think of the future you're scared.

By the time you turn 45, the wave rolling down your river will be a water wall one kilometre high. No wonder the digitalisation of our world makes us feel like we're drowning.

Why don't we sense its full pervasiveness?

The second remarkable feature of the Digital Revolution is its ubiquity: the river is flowing everywhere. Everyone is so connected that it's hard to distinguish where our body ends and our virtual reality begins.

Klaus Schwab, founder of the World Economic Forum, goes as far as to argue that we are seamlessly transitioning to an age where new technologies – such as robotics, artificial intelligence, biotechnology, 3D printing and autonomous vehicles – are fusing our physical, digital and biological worlds together. He, and others, call it the "Fourth Industrial Revolution".

Regardless of numbers and labels, our hyperconnected world is bringing interdependence to another level. The theory that *the flap of a butterfly's wings in Brazil can set off a tornado in Texas* has been around at least since the 1970s.[15] But in our world, where everything is wired up, connected, intertwined and interdependent, technological innovation spreads around the globe like magic.

It took the telephone 75 years to reach 50 million users. The radio needed 38 years, and the television just 13. And if four years seem like a short time for the internet to achieve the same target, what about nine months for Twitter and 19 days for Pokémon Go?[16]

This faster and faster uptake is changing society. It dramatically alters the way we interact, socially, economically and politically.

Just look at social networks like Twitter and the diffusion of mobile phones. They are the main force behind the speed at which political movements such as the Arab

Spring gain momentum across countries and borders.[17] Industries are now so connected that if an earthquake strikes Japan, US car manufacturers feel the impact on their supply chains almost at once, a top Ford executive told *The Economist*.[18] Everything sets off instant domino effects. Shocks in one industry can make another tremble, even if they seem completely unrelated.

A classic example is the disruption of the taxi and logistics industry in many countries, which was spurred by satellite-based Global Positioning Systems (GPS) and a proliferation of affordable smartphones. Without these technologies, digital delivery services and ridesharing platforms like Uber wouldn't have changed the way people and goods move around.

We sense this pervasiveness, but it is too intricate to comprehend. The interrelationships are effectively infinite, like those between neurons in the brain. But unlike the brain, anything can connect to anything else, and people have access to ideas from everywhere. We can't possibly grasp all these ties – and chains of ties – so we are partly at their mercy. Change occurs in startling ways and often with jarring force.

How did we get used to global awareness?

The Digital Revolution is also unprecedented because we can feel it all the time. No matter where we go, we can always be aware of everything that is happening everywhere else. We can attend a friend's wedding via Skype or watch the eruption of an Indonesian volcano live on Facebook. Modern technology puts our eyes, ears, and voice all over the globe.

As the philosopher Paul Virilio put it, "Today, everything is about speed and real time. We are no longer concerned with real space". The advantages are obvious.

For instance, we can now skip the commute to a grey office cubicle and work from a café or a beach thanks to cloud technology, wireless networks and mobile devices. Our car tells us automatically when to replace a faulty tire and how to avoid a traffic jam. Banking apps allow us to monitor our cash flow in real time on the go.

It's hard to switch off. When was the last time you ignored your smartphone for a few hours? We are overwhelmed by a flood of information, not just because the information is overwhelming, but because we keep staring at it.

In the 1970s, George Gerbner, an American journalist and academic famous for his research on mass media and communication, said television was making large parts of society suffer from what he called "Mean World Syndrome". He noticed that people who witnessed an ongoing stream of violent TV news and images develop a heightened sense of danger and mistrust, and perceive the world as mean.[19]

While Gerbner's diagnosis applied to traditional mass media, not modern social media, a growing body of literature signals that heavy use of social networks such as Facebook, Instagram and Twitter can lead to heightened anxiety and poor sleep. It's like watching *Jaws* and then going for a swim – with the image of a great white shark moving at the edge of your digitised goggles. We are in a constant state of shiver.

Smartphones and other connected devices now zoom riots from thousands of kilometres away right into our living rooms. We can sit on a balcony in the sun in our part of the world and still get unsettled by all sorts of terrible things happening around the globe – wars, terrorism, floods, scandals. It can make us feel precarious, even if we have nothing to worry about.

It has all crept up on us. From the first thrill of linking into the internet to the first emails from Brazil or Korea to the videos of tsunamis as they happen and friends chatting onscreen from once-exotic locales, we've slowly gotten used to what prior generations would have thought miraculous. We can see climbers on Mt. Everest in real time and make robots bow across the globe.

The world is right before us, and it is exhilarating and deeply worrisome.

It's time to calm down

With so much changing at once, it is only natural many of us are looking for an escape from a life in fast-forward. We join slow food movements. We buy artisan sourdough bread that takes 36 hours to prove. And hipsters from Sydney to London have made it a quirky habit to take photos not with their smartphones, but with clunky old-fashioned film cameras. It's a small analogue rebellion against the Digital Revolution.

Moore's Law tells us that technological change will keep accelerating on that ever-steeper upward curve. This means we can't return to a past where our careers, our savings and our futures were far more predictable than today. The calm river of decades ago is now that swift, complex, uncertain stream and we have yet to figure out how to navigate it.

But what if our perception is failing us more than our river-riding skill?

Take automation. The common narrative is that robots are stealing our jobs and that no one is safe. The forecasts are gloomy, but also wildly diverging. Some researchers estimate that automation jeopardises nearly every second job in the United States (47%); others say only 7 per cent of jobs are at risk. In Europe, the estimates range from 61 per cent to 5 per cent.[20]

Yes, this feels like looking at two different weather forecasts: one promising clear blue skies, the other lightning and torrents. How is this possible? Should we always pack an umbrella, just in case?

We find the answer – again – in Heraclitus' theory of opposites. Because where there's destruction, there must be creation. One cannot exist without the other. Knowing this should help us shift our perspective.

Labour markets are always in flux, and there's immense uncertainty over the actual impact of automation on future employment. Each year, around 20 per cent of jobs in a typical industrialised country are created or destroyed, according to the OECD.[21] Contrary to common belief, technology has created more jobs than it destroyed in recent years, we read in the latest World Bank analysis of European work trends.[22]

Sure, technology is substituting workers in some jobs, but "overall, it is raising labour demand", it says. Also: More than 85 per cent of job types we're about to see in 2030 do not even exist today, predicts the Institute for The Future, a US think tank, in a study commissioned by computer manufacturer Dell.[23]

Maybe the future is not all that bad. Maybe we have just gotten used to the constant flow of prophecies that pop up on our smartphones and predict the end of human work in the automation age.

Researchers from nearly every large economic institution say we'll lose some jobs due to automation, but fears that robots will cause mass unemployment are exaggerated. Machines can replace human workers only for predictable routine tasks that can be translated into the code language a computer understands.

Flipping hamburgers in a fast-food kitchen could be such a "codifiable" task. Or sifting through piles of files, entering data, scanning barcodes and driving mining trucks through the desert.

Machines struggle to perform unpredictable tasks or tasks that require uniquely human input. They struggle to reliably mimic human empathy and creativity and our ability to interpret complex situations. Computers may one day write a hit song, but it's much harder to imagine them inspiring people or persuading clients. As automation becomes more widespread, human workers will increasingly shift towards the uniquely human tasks that robots can't master.

The introduction of ATMs in the United States provides a classic example. When banks first started using these automatic money dispensers, the bank tellers who had until then handed out notes and coins to customers were fearful. They were afraid of losing their jobs to the new technology, which did their work cheaply and reliably.

The opposite happened. As automation lowered the total operating costs of running a bank, the financial institutions opened even more subsidiaries and hired more staff to run them. There were now more bank people at work, but they performed different tasks. Instead of the mind-numbing sorting, stacking and counting of bank notes, employees increasingly spent their time managing human relationships and giving financial advice.

The bottom line: Over the past 40 years, as automation accelerated, the number of tellers actually doubled in the US.[24] And that's not due to population growth; the US population increased by only two-thirds during this period.

Unfortunately, things don't always go smoothly. History is full of examples where new inventions, from the weaving machine to the internal combustion engine, displaced thousands of workers. It can be devastating for an individual. Yet centuries of history also show that job gains outweigh job losses in the long run, as technology gives birth to new opportunities.

If we trust this process of creative destruction, there will likely be enough jobs in the future. We just need to know how to get them.

Don't end up like Heraclitus

Times are turbulent and will continue to be. Are we ready for an increasingly unpredictable future? We have to ask ourselves fundamental questions.

Do we all need the mindset of millennial workers, many of whom have already adopted a completely different attitude towards work and stability? Are we like pebbles in the raging river being shaped by the elements? Should we try to redirect the water's flow? Or should we cease resisting forces we cannot stop?

Philosophers like Heraclitus have been telling us for ages that life is a constant flow. It has always been this way, only now technology is accelerating it so much faster and weaving it in extraordinary patterns. We think we have lost control over our world, when in fact we have lost our old world. Nothing ever stays the same, no river, no man, not us, not our lives, and there is no point weeping about it.

By the way, do you want to know what happened to Heraclitus?

While he understood that everything is always in flux, he himself mainly stood apart and watched it. When asked to take part in the political life of his hometown Ephesus, he declined and said he preferred to play knucklebones (an old-fashioned game like throwing dice) with children.

Eventually, Heraclitus retired completely from social life and moved into the mountains, where he dwelt as a hermit until he got sick. According to some ancient Greek historians, he self-prescribed an obscure treatment which involved "covering his body with manure and lying out in the sun to dry".

Heraclitus' end was tragic. He reportedly died trapped in a pile of dried excrement and eaten by dogs.[25] See where a life of lamentation and inaction may take you?

Let's start by looking at those who do well at riding the turbulence. Let's learn from those at the helm of companies that continue to thrive in a VUCA world.

These companies are on the river like us, and they must cope with its sudden, unpredictable changes. And they have at least two things in common.

For one, they are very lean and grow without many physical assets. Secondly, they are constantly reinventing themselves. For example, McKinsey research shows that the most profitable North American companies in recent years were the ones that invested heavily in intangible assets such as research patents, innovative production processes, brands and networks. These companies are hugely successful without accumulating a lot of machinery, factories or office space.[26]

In fact, they may not physically own anything.

They are light, so they can float better.

It's a bewildering corporate existence that US innovation expert Tom Goodwin has summed up poignantly:[27]

Uber, the world's largest taxi company, owns no vehicles. Facebook, the world's most popular media owner, creates no content. Alibaba, the most valuable retailer, has no inventory. And Airbnb, the world's largest accommodation provider, owns no real estate.

This observation can help us build a survival strategy for the liquid life. In the digital economy, knowing how to make things happen is becoming more important than owning things.

Research also shows that the most successful firms of our times remain nimble. They are light *and* flexible, constantly disrupting their own organisational structures and strategies before they can be disrupted. Take Amazon: it started as an online bookstore and it's now investing billions of dollars in producing original TV series and movies, as well as putting its bets on developping devices powered by AI.

Winners in these turbulent times know how to overcome the temptation of inertia. They flexibly re-allocate their resources and don't hesitate to change the status quo.[28] They have made it a habit to rebuild their boat and are continuously adjusting their route while sailing into unmapped waters.

In sum, they carry minimal weight from the past, and they react swiftly to a fast-changing world.

We can do that too.

When the music changes,
so does the dance.
– African proverb

Chapter 2

Say hello to the jagged career

From Manhattan to Manchester, from crisis-ridden Spain to mining-rich Australia, Western labour markets now show eerie similarities. If you still hold a traditional job – one that comes with an open-ended contract, a routine of five 8-hour work days per week, sick leave, holiday pay, and a business card that makes sense to your mum – you will soon be the odd one out.

"Normal work" is disappearing. Just ask Adrián, the Spanish video producer who is desperate to find a stable job and, despite his qualifications and experience, finds nothing but piecemeal employment: short-term, unpredictable and lacking in social security, yielding just enough money to pay the bills, with no cash cushion at the end of the month.

Then there's the opposite trend. Look at Alessandro, the Italian lawyer, who left a promising career in the corporate world, disillusioned and overworked. A desk slave turned free agent, not because he had to, but because he could. "I'd rather be kitesurfing," he told himself after realising that, with the right attitude and a remote internet access, the opportunities to reinvent your professional identity are endless today.

Adrián and Alessandro may have different motivations, but they share the same fate: for both, work has become a delicate balancing act between possibility and precarity.

Welcome to the *gig economy*.

What is the gig economy?

Let's start with "gig". What is it? Let's ask the Oxford English Dictionary, the accepted authority on the English language:

Gig (n.) /gɪg/
A job, especially one that is temporary or that has an uncertain future.

If you're at a party anywhere between San Francisco and Sydney, chances are you'll meet someone who "just landed a gig".

Speaking of "gigs" instead of "jobs" reveals a massive mindset shift. Unlike our parents' generation, we know that today's jobs won't last a lifetime. In its basic form, "gig" simply indicates that some sort of work opportunity has popped up in the speaker's life, an opportunity to earn income with a skill you're good at until a better offer comes along.

The gig economy is a world where stable, well-paid work is increasingly hard to come by. Where the boundaries blur between secure jobs and insecure gigs, between being employed and self-employed, between business owner and worker, between settled career and a life turned liquid. Where how you make a living no longer fits into a standard business card format. Where professional distinctions are hazy and job profiles can be bewildering.

In this new economy, people can be many things at once. They are part-time doctors *and* contract charter flight pilots *and* casual actors. They work as radio journalists during the week and teach yoga on weekends. They are physiotherapists in the morning and Uber drivers at night. They co-own a café, but they also sell their own music on Spotify or Bandcamp, on top of publishing a vegan food blog.

"My profile is multidisciplinary – which is a formal way of saying that I can do several things if needed," says Adrián. For him, life in the gig economy isn't a choice. An entire generation of people, no matter how well educated, is coming to terms with the fact that job uncertainty and "the sensation of living on the tightrope" is the new normal, writes Spanish newspaper *El País.*

In some regions of Southern Europe half of all youths remain unemployed and the share of under-34-year-olds still living with their parents has soared to around 80 per cent in recent years.[1] In Canada's latest census, almost 35 per cent of all young professionals said they were living at their parents' home, a new record.[2]

Joining a sprawling gig economy of casuals and contractors may be the only option to make ends meet. After all, a precarious job beats no job. And to a certain degree it's logical that young people earn less and don't get hired full-time immediately after finishing school or university. Most have no relevant work experience, so why should a company take the risk and employ them permanently?

However, the erosion of stable work is now sweeping. The phenomenon is spreading beyond the young and unskilled and beyond countries still grappling with the fallout from the Global Financial Crisis. We're witnessing a large-scale casualisation of working lives in every Western country, regardless of its economic health.

Freelancers are on track to become the majority of the American workforce by 2027, some studies suggest.[3] Zoom to Europe and you'll find that 42 per cent of all workers are freelancers, casuals, temporary staff or part-timers, up from 38 per cent in 2003.[4] "If this trend continues, standard contracts will only apply to a minority of workers within the next decade," warns the European Parliament.[5]

In the average OECD economy, one in six workers is now self-employed and a further one in eight is on a temporary contract.[6]

Numbers are rising.

In Canada, temporary contracts have doubled over the past three decades. In Germany, arguably the EU's strongest economy, temporary employment is at an all-time high.[7] In Britain, so-called "zero-hour contracts", which come with no guaranteed minimum working hours, have increased sharply.

For the first time in recorded history, the rate of permanent full-time employment in Australia has dropped below 50 per cent, even though the job market is booming and the economy hasn't seen a recession in almost three decades.[8]

And if you visit Amsterdam with its maze of waterways, bicycle lanes and beer bars, you'll be surprised to learn that the rate of full-time permanent employment in the Netherlands has slipped to 34 per cent.[9]

Let that sink in: only one out of three people in the Dutch workforce still holds an open-ended standard contract. The rest are part-timers, freelancers, casuals, contractors. Basically, the Netherlands *is* a gig economy.

Many of these people have voluntarily swapped the standard job for a freelance life sustained by a bunch of side hustles. They are part of a growing mass of digital creatives and nomadic laptop workers who embrace modern technology to live a life in flux, always online, on demand, ready to work anytime and anywhere – from a bullet train in Japan, a co-working space in San Francisco or a yoga retreat atop a Balinese mountain. Home, they say, is where the Wi-Fi is.

Yet for millions of others, the digital on-demand economy is evolving at a pace that is dazzling and daunting at the same time. The gig work trend remains unsettling because it typically tilts the power balance in favour of employers. Casual and temporary workers are often the first to be fired in a downturn. They tend to earn less and often miss out on social protection.

What's even more unsettling is that gig work is rising at a time of rapid technological advances in robotics and artificial intelligence. Lawyers can lose their jobs because of intelligent software. IBM's supercomputer Watson is said to outsmart any human doctor in diagnosing ailments. Who needs taxi, bus or truck drivers once autonomous cars go mainstream?

We can't shake the disturbing sense that we are fighting a lost battle and that machines might soon devour the few jobs that remain. Is this our future? Waking up every morning not knowing whether there will be enough work tomorrow to get by? Is job security a thing of the past? Precariously ever after?

It's ironic. As a society we are enjoying the highest living standards in history. But as individuals we face the greatest economic uncertainty in generations, as digital technology topples the steadfast principles that once guided our parents through life.

However, we know that workers have faced existential crises before: during times of war and famine, during the Industrial Revolution, during the Great Depression. Casual jobs have been around for ages, and so have our fears. Is it really all that bad? Can we shift things to our favour? And if so, how?

To answer these questions, we need to dig deeper. We need to first cut through the noise and have a look at the basics. Where did the gig economy come from? What are its inner workings? What is its future, and how can we step forward without being afraid of what's ahead?

A short history of precariousness

BLACK JAZZ AND BISMARCK

The gig economy has always been about precariousness. Its history is intrinsically linked to people trying to make ends meet, living day by day at the mercy of employers. Its roots reach deep into the early 20th century, to a time of brisk industrial growth and social progress across the Western world.

Substantial welfare reforms were spreading from Germany to Britain and later to the United States, inspired by the Prussian welfare state that Chancellor Otto von Bismarck had established to stifle social unrest in the new era of mass production.

More and more countries created safety nets for the poor. They introduced compulsory social security systems to insure workers against sickness, injury, disability and unemployment. Women received maternity protection and child labour became illegal.

Such achievements became the foundation for many modern developed economies. They made working lives more predictable for the majority. And they shunted the precarious life to the margins of society. To the immigrants. The unskilled. And the blacks.

In the United States legislators passed a progressive social reform agenda, but it had holes. Notably, it failed to cover black people. In the early 1920s, racial segregation was still legal, and employers openly discriminated against Afro-Americans. Their career options were largely limited to unskilled work in assembly lines or on farms, harvesting cotton, tobacco and sugar cane. Some turned to shadier moneymaking opportunities such as the numbers game, an illegal lottery racket played in poor and working-class neighbourhoods.

One of these underground entrepreneurs was Denver Ferguson, a young ambitious man who ran a small print shop in Indianapolis and, as a side hustle, operated a numbers game and churned out betting cards. Every day, he would send runners across town who secretly met gamblers in the back rooms of the tavern, the soft drink parlour, the barber, the laundry. Their main job was to collect money and betting cards with a three-digit number combination, known as "the gig".

By the mid-1920s, his underground business was flourishing. Looking for an outlet to invest his growing fortune, Ferguson spotted a niche: among Indiana's flickering nightclubs there was not a single venue for a black audience. He was determined to change things. Soon the runners were also acting as location and talent scouts, finding music venues and booking black entertainers on Ferguson's behalf. "I've got a gig for you," they would say, slowly changing the original meaning of the word.

The betting slips were gambles on the future – and so were the lives of black jazz musicians at the time. A tour meant travelling tiring distances between a string of venues in small American towns.

Some gigs paid just enough to keep a band's hopes up and buy a dinner of chitterlings, a poor man's pub dish made of pig intestines.

Denver Ferguson would later rise to fame as the kingpin of America's largest network of black jazz clubs: the Chitlin' Circuit. And while the origin of "gig" is not absolutely clear, the story suggests that this black businessman from Indianapolis played a key role in the birth of the early gig economy.[10]

THE FINE LINE BETWEEN GOOD AND BAD JOBS

The earliest gig workers came from the fringes of society. They were getting by on a song, with no safety net, shut out of the social security system.

Much has changed since then.

The US abolished their racial segregation policies. Labour unions curbed the power of corporations and carved out more worker rights. Workers gained stronger legal protections. The 40-hour work week was introduced. France lowered the retirement age to 58 years. Societies became more liberal. More women joined the labour market in pursuit of professional careers. A record number of young people finished higher education.

When our parents' generation left high school, the world of work seemed clear-cut. Thanks to the modern welfare state, it seemed easy to avoid precariousness. If you chose the right education and occupation, were committed and hard-working, you could expect to find a secure, predictable, well-paying job. You could expect to afford health insurance, a pension plan and a bank credit to buy a car, a house and your wedding rings.

The social security achievements of the past few decades didn't eradicate precarious work. But most developed countries had put enough institutional safeguards in place to prevent a large number of workers from sliding into poverty and exploitation. A lot of precarious jobs went underground where they fuelled shadow economies.

**

Precarious workers were people like Wladimir from Ukraine, whom Vera met one chilly winter morning on the outskirts of Cologne between a highway shoulder and a scrapyard.

He was tiptoeing around empty oil canisters and old tyres in the predawn with a bunch of other illegal immigrants. There was the sound of scrunching gravel and rumbling Slavic words. She was a reporter writing an investigative feature for a German newspaper. Wladimir was waiting for a pick-up truck to come and hurry him away in the twilight to wherever someone with strong hands and little German was needed: to tile a bathroom floor, bend steel on a construction site, heave buckets of cement.

Wladimir had fine hands and witty eyes. In Ukraine, he was a philosophy student. In Germany he was happy to do backbreaking work and line up with other dark figures on the side of the road like a prostitute. He earned just a few euros per day cash in hand – money he'd take back home to finance his studies. Several construction companies, some of them big and well-known, were happy to hire these shadow workers. It was illegal, of course, but convenient. It helped employers lower their overall labour costs because for a day labourer like Wladimir they didn't have to pay tax or social security contributions.

That morning, Wladimir waited in vain. No pick-up truck came and that meant: no work. Vera agreed to give him a lift back to the place where he stayed, a tall, mustard-coloured apartment tower he shared with a few fellow countrymen.

Would he have enough money for breakfast? He pointed at her mobile phone. "Zappzarapp," he said and made a snatching gesture. It was neither German nor Ukrainian, but Vera understood. If things got tough, Wladimir would go pickpocketing to survive.

***

Where do you draw the line between a good job and a bad job? When does a job become a gig? And when does a gig become a fight for survival?

Precarious work is a relative concept. There is no globally accepted definition. It is a politicised term that is often used subjectively to describe vulnerable workers who have an insecure job and few entitlements to receive income support.

The European Parliament, in a recent attempt to reach a common understanding, says "work that is characterised by a lack of control over job content, lack of autonomy, lack of employee voice, low variation of tasks, or a lack of control over working time carries a higher degree of precariousness".[11] In other words, if you lose control of your career and are at the mercy of employers, you have moved deeper into the zone of precariousness.

Casual work has always existed. But in the past, the boundaries between casual work and precarious work seemed much clearer. Casual workers were typically students, pensioners or housewives. They worked a few hours here and there to earn pocket money or prop up their pension. During high school, we all had casual jobs. We worked as babysitters, stacked supermarket shelves or trekked through the neighbourhood to deliver the local advertising gazette. We were waitressing, serving customers in the lottery shop, clipping a nightclub's marketing flyers behind car wipers, vacuum-cleaning parking garages or promoting pet food in the pedestrian mall.

Pensioners often enjoy casual jobs. A retired gardener would drop by every so often at Vera's parents' house to prune the pear tree until the gaps between the branches were wide enough for him to flick his hat through. Her mother-in-law, a few months after receiving her first pension, took up a gig as a call-centre agent for an online fashion retailer. She got paid for talking customers through dress sizes and return policies, two mornings per week.

The services industry would collapse without casual workers. But there is a difference between doing casual work on your own terms and on others'. In the past, few people would have considered casual work a serious career choice. It wasn't something you'd do in earnest. It was a way you could gain some extra money and a flavour of life. Vera's retired mother-in-law enjoyed her call-centre work because it kept her busy and she had colleagues to chat to, but when she had enough, she quit.

Some casual jobs could earn you bragging rights. Hero stories to be retold for years to come. Like the one of a friend's friend who, dressed up as a rabbit, was paid to hand out leaflets to Saturday shoppers on behalf of a recycling company. He lasted a few hours, then got side-tracked. The manager found him later stretched out on the pavement in his rabbit costume, drunk but happy.

It used to be the nature of a casual job: you'd do it casually. Like the Australian friend who was paid to drive the sand cleaning machine in between greyhound races. It got him through university, and he admittedly smoked a lot of weed at the time. "Mate, you had to be stoned to do that kinda job," he said.

The here and now: Gig work goes mainstream

CASUAL WORK HAS STOPPED BEING CASUAL

What if casual work stops being casual? There are mounting accounts of people who seem to have lost control over their working lives. They are packing and stocking and wrapping consumer goods in the giant warehouses of online retailers. Or they heave them in and out of delivery trucks and drive them to people's homes. It's blue-collar work for those who lack the skills to do something else.

The internet has made online retail a huge business. Food delivery is booming. Today's delivery drivers work for tech startups with funky names such as Deliveroo, Foodora or Uber Eats. They speed through dangerous city traffic on their own motorbikes, self-insured and getting drenched by the rain.

Let's be honest, delivery drivers have been around for decades and it's never been a dream job. They now use smartphones and geolocation services, but other than that, their work conditions have barely changed. Still, there's one important difference: today, this job has become a primary source of income for millions of people with no hero story to tell.

Investigators have uncovered endless cases of casual worker exploitation. They reveal that the delivery industry has become an opaque web of large corporations, contractors and subcontractors, who often employ their couriers as "independent agents" – with no maternity benefits and sick leave, no paid holidays and no employer contribution to their pension fund.

In London, a freelance driver for delivery service DPD collapsed and died after missing hospital appointments to treat his diabetes because the company threatened to fine him for a day's absence. In Chicago, a pregnant driver for ridesharing app Lyft continued to work even as she went into labour. A Canadian economist calculated that UberX drivers in Australia routinely earn less than the minimum wage.[12]

FALSE FREELANCERS, REAL TROUBLE

A string of court cases around the globe has ensnared firms such as Amazon, Hermes, Uber, Foodora and Deliveroo for allegedly fuelling what is known as "bogus", or "sham", self-employment. Labour unions accuse them of breaching labour laws by misrepresenting workers as independent contractors when in fact they are working like regular employees – just for shoddier pay and without a social safety net.

People in sham self-employment rely heavily on one company as their main, often only, source of income. Employers can exploit this dependency, set terms as they please and tell workers to "take it or leave it".

Many gig workers feel they don't have a choice. A British Parliament inquiry into the practices of delivery services accused companies of propagating "a myth of self-employment" and denying workers basic rights out of greed.[13]

"I had no control over anything that I ever did," one former Hermes courier told the inquiry, adding he was threatened with "service removal" if he didn't play by the rules.[14]

Politicians from Canada to France are now rushing to adjust outdated labour laws to the reality of the modern gig economy. Their goal is to prevent digital platform companies from exploiting workers.

But the gig economy is only the tip of the iceberg. App-based ridesharing and delivery services have simply accelerated an existing trend towards insecure work. Companies in all corners of the world and across all industries are replacing permanent staff with contractors, freelancers or casuals, often simply to bypass social security obligations.

Germany, for example, is close to full employment, but working conditions are deteriorating for many. A string of employers, including some of the largest retailers, have opted out of enterprise agreements with unions that oblige them to pay a minimum wage.

Almost every second worker in the country now holds a job in which minimum wage rules don't apply anymore, according to labour union statistics.[15]

Publishing groups have moved entire newsrooms into this grey zone. They have laid off thousands of reporters, editors and photographers, then offered some of them their old job back – as freelancers, paid per article and with no social security. You could argue that mass layoffs are justified as the media industry struggles with a structural shift from print to online news.

However, the push towards precarious contract work and sham self-employment is occurring on a broad scale. It is not confined to troubled industries or low-skilled workers.

For instance, in Spain, a multilingual psychologist friend with a PhD and international work experience was struck when her boss made everyone in his small neurolinguistic services firm redundant. "You can continue to work for me," he said, "but I would only rehire you as a contractor and you would need to pay me if you want to use my medical equipment."

WORKING (TOO) LITTLE, WORKING POOR?

When does part-time and contract work become a problem? There is none if workers are adequately compensated. Some people deliberately work fewer hours because they are studying, have young children, are overworked or generally seeking a better work-life balance. They accept part-time or temporary jobs because they can afford it, if only for a limited time.

If you are a management consultant in London earning £150 an hour, you may as well work less and enjoy life. But if you live in Madrid and, like Adrián, simply cannot find a stable well-paying job, you will be desperate to work more and willing to accept precarious gig work to supplement your income.

In the US, millions of people are doing just that. Known as "working poor", they plough through double shifts in low-paid casual jobs, pouring coffee at doughnut shops in the morning and serving diet coke in roadside diners at night to stay above the poverty line.

As the gig economy expands, many are afraid that Europe is poised to share America's fate. Underemployment has become a burning issue across all major Western economies. It describes a trend of working fewer hours than you'd like because there is no alternative. Economists warn that "underemployment is the new unemployment" because it has been quietly rising,

43

even in countries where the official jobless rate is low.[16] In 2017, nine million part-time workers in the European Union – that's every fifth – would have preferred to work more.[17] These people are disproportionately female, young, less educated, on temporary contracts and in elementary occupations. In the US, they are also commonly black, Hispanic or unincorporated self-employed.[18]

In Mediterranean crisis countries from Greece to Portugal, involuntary part-time work has skyrocketed over the past decade, and young people are most affected. In Italy alone, 80 per cent of all under 30-year-olds who worked part-time in 2016 did so because they could not find a permanent full-time job.[19]

There are similar problems with contract work, which in Europe has increased so rapidly that officials warn it may signal an "overexploitation of fixed-term contracts".[20] Six out of 10 European temporary workers reported in 2014 that they were on a fixed-term contract because they could not find a permanent job.[21]

HOW FRIGHTENED SHOULD WE BE?

The gig economy of the past century has made a comeback. Once, only those at the edge of society faced the struggle to get by on insecure, short-term employment with an uncertain future. Today everyone is at risk of becoming a gig worker.

Gig work has gone mainstream. It has moved from the fringes to the heart of society.

The issue is real, but how frightened should we be? Newspapers tend to overplay the drama in human lives. Emotional stories sell. Bad news is good news, they say. But what if there is more good news in the bad news than we can see? There are strong signs that the gig work trend is here to stay. Does this mean we'll all end up on the brink of poverty? Enough people prove the opposite, and we'll feature some of them in detail in the second half of this book. They are defying what seems like a fatal slide into precariousness. They stack the odds in their favour by going with the tide of technological change, instead of against it.

These pioneers of the Flow Generation understand that when the music changes, so does the dance. They understand that the gig economy is here to stay. And when you can't change something, you have to adapt.

Why the gig economy is here to stay

The gig economy with its surge in atypical, casual, freelance, contract, part-time and self-employed work will unlikely reverse back to the neat nine-to-five job routine of past decades.

Four factors prevent a return to the predictable work reality that our parents had gotten used to.

First, an unabated crisis mentality still heavily influences corporate hiring and investment decisions. Second, the boom in the services industry, where hiring has always been more unpredictable and cyclical, ensures that demand for temporary, contract and casual workers remains high.

Third, remote working technology and the emergence of digital platforms have led to a cultural shift in the corporate world: from outsourcing to crowdsourcing on demand. Fourth, a growing number of workers, particularly those who are part of the millennial generation, are voluntarily escaping fixed contracts and routines.

Let's have a look at why this is so and what it means for the future.

STUCK IN CRISIS MENTALITY

The collapse of investment bank Lehman Brothers in 2008 set off a series of events that rocked the global economy, and we still feel its repercussions today. What happened back then can help explain why standard jobs are now in permanent decline.

Lehman's bankruptcy was the most expensive in the history of the US. It unravelled a gigantic mortgage gamble that had ensnared banks around the world and caused stock markets, property prices and companies globally to crash. By 2010, more than 8 million people in the developed world had lost their jobs, 25,000 alone at Lehman Brothers.[22]

To soften the blow of the crisis, many unemployed people started "gigging", often working several casual or part-time jobs wherever they could. They thought of gigs as stop-gap solutions until markets returned to calm. However, a decade later it's clear the gig economy is more than a blip. It is, according to some commentators, "a seismic shift in the world of work on par with the advent of the assembly line, or even the weekend"[23].

One reason for the persistence of the gig economy is a profound shift in corporate thinking. During the crisis years many companies developed a wait-and-see mentality. They shelved longer-term business plans, reined in costs and postponed investments. They also refrained from hiring anyone they wouldn't be able to get rid of in a flash in case the crisis deepened.

Fixed-term contracts became a favourite hiring tool. Several European countries, including Italy, Germany and Belgium, had already liberalised labour laws in the years prior to the crisis in an attempt to combat youth unemployment and shadow work. They introduced a variety of new ultra-flexible non-standard employment contracts to encourage hiring – contracts that would end after six months or leave workers "on call" with no guaranteed work hours.

When the Global Financial Crisis hit, short-term hiring soared. Companies in France, Italy and elsewhere got into the habit of replacing permanent staff with workers on very short temporary contracts. The tool to help young people enter the labour market faster now applied to workers of all ages, often with decades of experience.

Temporary contracts spread like an epidemic. By 2012, three-quarters of new hires in Portugal, Spain, Poland and the UK had signed a fixed-term contract.[24]

Today, the brunt of the crisis has faded, yet hiring policies remain stuck in crisis mode. This is fanning the growth of the gig economy.

It is one explanation for why atypical employment across the developed world is now growing faster than standard employment – and will continue to. Employers, particularly in Southern Europe, have gotten used to the payoffs of fixed-term contracts, which carry low risks for them and high risks for workers. When layoffs are inevitable, temporary employees are usually the first to go. Companies don't even have to fire them. They simply refuse to renew the contracts.

THE HOLLYWOOD MODEL OF HIRING

It's an illusion to think that we can stop this trend towards more on-call work and fixed-term contracts. We can't. The services economy in our industrialised Western world continues to show rapid growth, and this buoys gig work. As Asian low-cost manufacturers have begun to champion the mass production of cars, clothes and electronics, companies in developed countries are changing their focus to high-margin services. This shift is another reason why the gig economy will get larger, not smaller. The on-call work trend is here to stay, even if governments decide to reverse ultra-flexible labour laws or succeed in reining in sham self-employment in the delivery industry.

Flexible hiring has always underpinned the services industry. In retail and hospitality, where customer demand can be fickle, employers rely heavily on shop assistants, chefs, bartenders, waitresses or hotel receptionists to be available ad hoc. It's a similar situation in the professional business service sector, which comprises a raft of occupations – consultants, architects, legal advisers, accountants, IT security providers, web designers and other creatives.

Professional business services are growing fast, as goods production continues to decline in many advanced economies.[25] Work in these industries is highly client-driven and often revolves around short-term projects, for which companies draw on a mix of in-house talents and highly specialised contractors.

It's inevitable that, as professional services become more important, short-term project-based work will increase. In the future, a growing number of employers will behave like movie producers who hire actors, make-up artists, cameramen, catering crews and screenwriters for the duration of just one large gig.

Some call it the 'Hollywood model' of hiring.

DIGITAL PLATFORMS: SUPERHERO FOR HIRE

Technology is the backbone of the modern gig economy. It is the third factor that's hindering us from a return to the comfort of predictable working days any time soon. In less than 100 years the internet has replaced Denver

Ferguson's gig men, who crisscrossed the streets of Indianapolis in search of saxophone players, singers and other jazz musicians.

Today, startups with names such as PeoplePerHour, Freelancer and Taskrabbit have become the new talent scouts. They run on digital platforms that act as match-makers between gig workers and paying clients. Such platforms have popped up everywhere from Toronto to Tel Aviv in recent years.

Much like Ferguson's runners or old-fashioned newspaper classifieds, they alert anyone willing to do short-term, casual work when an opportunity comes up. But digital platforms are much more effective than the artist booking agents or job noticeboards of the past. Within fractions of a second, they can mobilise and connect millions of people worldwide – thanks to soft-ware algorithms, geolocation technology, and the ultra-fast wireless internet.

The speed, convenience and low cost at which these gig work platforms make all sorts of services available explain their explosive growth. Some of these gig platforms provide physical household services for a local area. You can click through a site like Airtasker and find a handyman who drops by for a couple of hours to assemble your new Ikea bed. You can open the smartphone apps of ride-hailing services Uber or Lyft on your phone and find a driver who chauffeurs you to the airport in his private car. Or you can order a Thai curry for dinner and a Deliveroo driver will deliver it to your doorstep.

Yet a large and rising share of gig work is invisible these days. It is just as transient as a pizza delivery gig, but workers can do it online and from anywhere in the world.

Dozens of digital platforms now cater for just that type of online gig. They represent a highly flexible and highly skilled crowd of independent professionals who are always on call to master a specialist task that a company is either unable or unwilling to perform with its own staff.

Think of an architectural practice that needs a pile of construction drawings done overnight to meet a deadline. An e-commerce startup that needs speedy legal advice for a one-off cryptocurrency transaction. Or a graphic design firm that needs a visual animation expert to create a motion graphic for a special client project.

Digital platforms make a whole new breed of talent available to employers: a high-tech version of the day labourer. Digital platform technology guarantees that a company that needs ad-hoc professional support will find it because someone in some time zone somewhere will always be available for it.

The gig economy is an employer's dream, and that's exactly how Upwork, one of the world's largest gig work platforms, is advertising the 12 million freelancers it represents:[26]

> You can think of them like a superhero who only comes in when you need help. They're not part of your staff. And you aren't responsible for providing them continuous work. You never control when, where, or how the work is done. You simply tell them what you need done (e.g., create a mobile app with a specific functionality), then step aside and wait for the deliverables. This means no training and no supervision.

Economists consider digital platforms a "hidden labour market phenomenon" because they still only account for a tiny share of the overall gig economy with its growing mass of short-term, on-call workers. One of the most comprehensive surveys to date on gig work in Europe suggests that only one in 10 people in the United Kingdom, in the Netherlands and in Germany have ever used a digital platform to find paid work.[27] In Southern Europe the share is higher. In Italy, for example, every fifth person has already earned some money via gig work platforms, according to the study.

The platform economy may still be in its infancy, but it is expanding rapidly. Researchers from the University of Oxford have begun to track all digital projects posted on the six largest English-language gig platforms worldwide and noticed a "dramatic spurt" in popularity. In just one year, from mid-2016 to mid-2017, the amount of gig work posted per day on these platforms increased by 26 per cent.[28]

FROM OUTSOURCING TO CROWDSOURCING

The rise of the gig and platform economy is unavoidable if you think about it. It is the natural evolution of the "I'm-working-from-home" trend.

Technological progress has already removed the need to do a standard desk job from a desk and thinned out corporate offices. Equipped with laptops, smartphones and wireless internet, everyone is now "on call" 24/7.

We work in our beds, on the train, on the plane, in taxis, in cafés, from a friend's kitchen table, under a beach umbrella or in a ski hut in the mountains. We save our files in the cloud, share our computer screens remotely, and simultaneously edit a document with colleagues on different continents. We can join a videoconference from a park bench and use a camera-supported mobile app to fill in an expense claim or tax return on the go.

51

Working from anywhere anytime has become so normal that many companies have introduced "hot desk" policies under which each chair, each desk is shared property. Employees who still bother to come into the office are forced to renegotiate their personal working space every morning on a first-come-first-served basis.

Rapid advances in automation technology and robotics are now pushing this remote work trend to the extreme. Automation has put us on a path of no return towards an ultra-dispersed workforce.

Every new machine, every piece of intelligent software in our workplaces will give employers a rationale to question the need for permanent, full-time, in-house staff. A growing number of startup teams work entirely location-independent, scattered around the globe with no headquarters.

Remember the time when pretty much every large corporation in the Western world outsourced entire jobs to India or the Philippines? Today, companies resort to *crowdsourcing*. They split jobs into a string of microtasks and then look for many different specialists to get each task done. This approach makes sense in the automation age. Machines can now perform many routine procedures faster and cheaper than we can, which encourages employers to rethink exactly when, how and where they still need humans to produce a good or service.

The future will look like this: employers will pull apart every job into automatable and non-automatable tasks and adjust their hiring accordingly. The result will be a hollowed-out corporate workforce, held together by just a skeleton of permanent staff and propped up by a large and fluctuating crowd of external gig workers. This contingent "always-ready" workforce – a mix of traditional freelancers, contractors, crowd workers and on-call workers – will perform the piecemeal of tasks that was once a full-time job.

Crowdsourcing is cheaper than outsourcing. Companies that use the traditional outsourcing model and move jobs to a low-cost location can save about 25 to 30 per cent of costs. Yet if they deconstruct jobs and then find the best resource for each task, they can save up to 80 per cent, according to estimates.[29]

Why should companies go back to the old employment models if they can do better with digital platforms, gig workers and machines? They won't.

The technology-driven gig economy carries the promise of hassle-free hiring with relatively few obligations for employers. No need to set up expensive call centres or other infrastructure abroad, no need to add anyone to the payroll, no need to figure out exotic labour laws in foreign countries. Many location-independent digital workers are not tied to an office desk. They set their own work schedule, often pay for their own social security and charge only for the output they produce – per hour or for the limited duration of a project.

In recent years, firms around the world have been adding significant numbers of freelancers, contractors and gig workers to their workforces and they will continue to, according to Deloitte research.[30] More than half of over 900 companies surveyed globally by consultancy Willis Towers Watson said digital and automation technology will enable them to hire more contingent workers by 2020.[31]

Contractors, freelancers and project workers already outnumber permanent employees in many industries, not just in Hollywood. A typical mining or energy company hires up to 80 per cent of its workforce as contractors. Many creative joints, including fashion magazines, have long employed more freelancers than full-time staff. That's not new.

What's new is that automation and digital technology is now enticing a league of other companies to follow suit, particularly those who rely on innovative products to keep an edge in their markets. The world's largest videogame makers, software producers, electronics manufacturers and consumer goods companies have begun to harness the collective brainpower of the gig work crowd – not just to update their websites, but to tackle some of their trickiest business challenges.

Many tap gig work platforms for fresh ideas. On Innocentive, a crowdsourcing platform, one of America's biggest plastics manufacturers recently awarded $30,000 to anyone who could "improve the state-of-the-art of 3D printing speed using polyolefins". Clothing manufacturers tap into platforms such as 99Designs or DesignCrowd to keep up with the fast fashion demand for new prints and designs each season. And if a company's own IT people struggle to crack complex code-writing tasks, they ask for help on Topcoder, a crowdwork platform with more than one million members worldwide.

PRECARIOUS AND HAPPY?

The increase in short-term, unpredictable employment is also getting tailwind from workers themselves, and this fact is somewhat hidden in the statistics. A surprisingly large number of people are gigging out of choice, not necessity. These people ensure that the gig economy will continue to grow at the expense of standard office jobs.

True, companies have pushed millions of workers, particularly in Southern Europe, into precarious employment and many of them are desperate to return to the world of secure, open-ended full-time jobs. But there is also a growing counter-pull from freelancers, part-timers and contract workers who have voluntarily cut the corporate ties.

McKinsey estimates that 70 per cent of the combined 162 million "independent workers" in the US and Europe – defined as people with a high degree of autonomy, who are paid by task, assignment or sales and usually have short-term relationships with their employer – are actively choosing this lifestyle because they like it.[32] A fresh Boston Consulting Group survey of 11,000 workers in 11 countries comes to the same conclusion.[33]

These "free agents" wear their autonomy like a badge. They are people like Alessandro, who at some point in their career decide to flow with the turning tide in labour markets, free themselves of the shackles of the corporate world and use digital technology to shape their own working lives. They would shun the label "gig worker" because it now refers almost exclusively to exploitative, precarious work. Yet they essentially make a living with gigs: short-term, unpredictable, insecure.

Are they precarious or happy or both? Precariously happy? The lines are blurred.

US economists Cheryl Carleton and Mary Kelly have studied the phenomenon and found that independent contractors and self-employed workers are more satisfied than people in regular jobs.[34] "These workers are seemingly willing to forego employer-provided benefits for greater flexibility and control," they write in a recent research paper.

***

Robert Crocker calls it the "corner office test". Not that he coined the term, but it's stuck with him: How much life are you sacrificing in pursuit of a glorified corner office? His previous job, working as a data visualisation specialist in a busy consulting firm in San Francisco, didn't pass the test. It was a competitive role. An enviable position. But Robert, then 27, thought the price of the corporate life was too high.

He had heard of the Dynamite Circle, a community of nomadic entrepreneurs who prove that anyone can work from anywhere these days. Robert, inspired by the success stories of these people, hatched a plan. Given that he was already working from cafés several times a week, why not work from cafés in the tropics? When his firm couldn't find a way to make the remote model work, Robert quit and moved to Bali on his own accord.

Finding clients was harder than he thought. For months he just lived on the bonus he had earned, refining his website, talking to other freelancers, drinking turmeric-spiced coffee during laptop breaks in one of Bali's many coworking spaces. Now, settled as a remote contractor with a large American IT company, he typically works 12-hour days. But when he rides his sandy scooter across the rice fields near Canggu beach, he feels more inspired than he ever was in San Francisco. "Regardless of your company's budget, it's hard to compete with the beaches of Bali", he says.

***

The pull from freedom-loving younger workers is powerful and has begun to put pressure on employers. "Remote work was once a corporate 'perk'. Now it's a mandatory requirement," says Liam Martin, co-founder of Running Remote in Bali, an annual conference for managers overseeing globally dispersed work teams. "It's a trend from the bottom up, led by millennials who have grown up with a laptop in their face." Martin's own company Time Doctor runs like that, too. The firm has no headquarters, only people working from wherever and whenever they like: 90-odd staff scattered over 28 countries. Martin himself is based in Ottawa. He sells software that helps like-minded firms coordinate their teams.

In the US, every second millennial worker is now freelancing, more than in any other generation before.[35] They value independence more highly than a presence on a corporate payroll. They hate feeling tied down. Over 40 per cent of millennials surveyed globally by Deloitte say they expect to leave their employer within a couple of years to do something different.[36]

Most millennials want to join the gig economy, and not just because it promises freedom, according to Deloitte. Six out of ten are convinced they can earn more money in the gig economy than in traditional employment.

***

The freelance and gig economy is growing so fast that it has mobilised a large grassroots movement of new startups and service providers. The second half of this book will shed more light on these firms and their solutions that help us stay afloat in this loose new world: health insurances, pension funds and banks that offer bespoke social security products for freelancers. Algorithmic job-hunting services. And co-living and coworking spaces for the modern location-independent professional.

There is an infinite difference between a Robespierre
who occurs only once in history
and a Robespierre who eternally returns,
chopping off French heads.
—Milan Kundera

Chapter 3

A night in the penthouse:
The sharing economy

L et's try this," Toby Frankenstein said one night over
dinner, and the silence that followed made his wife
Inbal wonder if he could hear her heart pound. Their 2-
year old son was fast asleep already, lulled by the
muffled clanking of the dishwasher, worlds away from
the mad tech rush of the San Francisco Bay Area, the
Silicon Valley where Toby worked in a secure and well-
paid IT role.

That night, he had come home with a beaming look
that he couldn't shake off. An upstart ridesharing firm
had offered him a job. Risky, yes, but promising. He'd
swap a pay cut and loss of job security for a career twist
and some startup stock options. It would be a bet on the
sharing economy.

"Let's try it," Toby repeated. In a few years, they
might be able to buy a house – if things went well.

What if they didn't? Inbal was hesitant. She had
grown up in a kibbutz in Israel and seen firsthand how

quickly the enthusiasm about collaborative consumption can wane. She had fond childhood memories of life in a community where everything belonged to everybody: cars, toys, food. Long dusty summer days spent playing on communal grounds framed by vegetable patches, pomegranate trees and pink bougainvillea.

As a child, Inbal went shopping without a wallet. The supermarket lady would take out a pencil and adjust the family balance in her notebook. Nobody in the kibbutz had a bank account. The collective paid for everything they needed, even for holidays or university fees. Everybody earned the same salary, regardless of their job in the community.

But over time, the system revealed cracks. Capitalism and globalisation began to challenge this way of life. Many of Inbal's friends felt starved of choice. The cities seemed to offer more goods, bigger houses and better career opportunities. Plagued by financial problems and an exodus of members, several kibbutzim opted for privatisation. In 2010, only one-quarter of the around 170 kibbutzim in Israel were still run communally, according to a study by Haifa University.

Inbal herself moved out after her military service. She never looked back. But now, at the dinner table with Toby, whom she had followed to San Francisco in pursuit of her own American Dream, she felt like a time traveller. The rapid rise of the modern sharing economy catapulted her back into the past and made her question the future.

And yet more and more people were getting job offers like Toby's. That's because a collaborative consumption craze has gripped people from the Western world to Asia. We all seem to have become sharers and borrowers. Were her fears unfounded?

Renting Hermes handbags and Lhasa Apsos

Everything you can imagine is now available to share, swap, or recycle. We share our lives on Instagram and Facebook like we share files. We share our skills on gig work platforms, and we share our possessions with strangers.

Collaborative consumption has become a mass phenomenon that is growing exponentially and well beyond momentum from the crisis. Since 2010, the cumulative funding for asset-sharing startups has skyrocketed from 100 million dollars to more than 23 billion.[1]

Digital sharing platforms rattle everything and everyone: taxi drivers and transport providers, fashion producers, tools and equipment makers, hoteliers and delivery services. One in six Americans used a sharing service in 2017.[2] Millions of others are ready to join. In a recent Nielsen survey, more than half of all respondents in Spain, Italy and Greece said they want to participate in collaborative consumption initiatives.[3]

Today, we can use someone's holiday house for a weekend, hire a gallery painting for a month, rent a designer handbag for a week, even borrow a pet (Lhasa Apso puppies anyone?) for a few hours. When your cellphone battery is running on empty in China, you can pick up a power bank at a public train station and drop it off at another one once your phone is charged, thanks to startups like Xiaodian and Laidian. You can do the same with umbrellas should you get caught in a sudden thunderstorm.

In 2011, a startup from New York seriously created a toilet sharing app hoping to strike gold with the idea that people would open their private bathrooms to random city folks desperate to find a clean place to pee. Except they wouldn't. The toilet app went down the drain.

The boundaries between mine and yours are fluid and "access is the new ownership", says author Rachel Botsman, a leading expert on the sharing economy.

Why?

In these precarious times, our cities are getting more crowded, our houses smaller, our cash flows less predictable – and our consumer habits are changing. Whether we need a car, a lawn mower or a place to stay, today we think twice if it's worth buying. It's not only about the hard cash you pay. Henry David Thoreau, the American writer, once said that "the price of anything is the amount of life you pay for it": the time and the headspace worrying about it, repairing it, making sure it's safe.

Every day, people around the globe are now making this calculation. And more and more are reaching the conclusion that ownership is overrated. They simply cannot be bothered to own stuff anymore because they may find everything they need in what American entrepreneur Lisa Gansky calls "the Mesh" – a wealth of new businesses whose core offerings are products and services to share.

Mesh businesses are radically transforming our lives and the way we interact with each other, and their reach is rapidly expanding globally.

They range from bike sharing and home swapping platforms to peer-to-peer lenders, energy cooperatives, and open source design firms. Mesh businesses throw the old formula of exclusive consumption out the window. Instead, they use social media, wireless networks, and data crunched from every available source to provide people with goods and services at the exact moment they need them, without the burden and expense of owning them outright, writes Gansky. These startups and digital platforms allow us to share cars and parking spaces, helping us save time and money.

In four out of five American cities, it's now cheaper to hitch a ride with Uber every day than to keep your own a car, according to investment firm Kleiner Perkins.[4] Italy alone counted nearly 150 different bicycle sharing programs in 2016.[5]

Can we trust this sharing boom? Inbal is not the only one asking this question, as the clear boundaries that once defined our lives blur on an unprecedented scale. Today, anyone can be both a tenant and a landlord, a consumer and a producer. We downsize and share, and yet we gain. But even back then some observers thought the sharing trend had become a bubble. How much further could it go before it popped?

Rise and fall forever

Cyclicality is a cornerstone of economics. Most of the founding fathers of modern economic theory incorporated business cycles and fluctuations into their thinking, including Keynes, Marx and Schumpeter, who identified four phases: expansion, crisis, recession and recovery.

Looking at the last two centuries of economic history, it's easy to agree with this theory, and apply it to how we make, trade and consume goods. It means anything that glows too bright too fast should make us wary. It may turn out to be a fad and fizzle out before we know it. What then should we make of the explosive trend of sharing things?

Economists think in cycles. One could be tempted to think that collaborative consumption belongs to an archaic past when people had to live in tribes to better hunt, gather berries, cultivate food – and probably to survive. And that in our modern times, we'd only drop our individualistic consumption if we had to.

The Spanish sociologist Manuel Castells explains the rebirth of collaborative consumption with the "culture of the crisis" which gripped our societies along with the economic meltdown that started in 2008. The Global Financial Crisis fuelled the sharing economy as much as the gig economy: we turned to sharing models because there was no other way to maintain our lifestyle.

Studies confirm that people are more willing to share and that social networking in communities rises when resources are scarce.[6] "People share only when they are unable to afford goods individually, and sharing practices decline once enough wealth is acquired for ownership," the World Economic Forum stated.[7]

Following this thinking, we could expect that the mass of consumers will eventually lose interest in all the sharing platforms that have emerged over the past decade. That all this enthusiasm about carpooling, house-swapping and peer-to-peer lending will gradually fade once the wounds of the Great Financial Crisis have healed.

History shows that recent episodes of collaborative consumption – think the kibbutz movement in Israel or community gardens in Europe – were indeed always limited to small groups of friends, families, or neighbours and only expanded during periods of scarcity sparked by war, mass migration or economic depression.

So where are we in this cycle? It's a critical question because in our precarious times, many of us see the sharing economy not only as a way to save money, but also as a supplemental source of income. Families around the world are making long-term financial decisions based on this trend. They count on covering part of their home loans or their kids' tuition fees by renting out rooms on Airbnb or by joining new peer-to-peer lending platforms that rely on a mass of like-minded members to function.

It may be too early to tell whether this means we have recovered completely from decades of debt-fuelled hyperconsumption. What is clear is that the explosive sharing economy is an enormous opportunity. It can help us build a life raft as we try to stay afloat in precarious times.

However, to fully harness these opportunities in a world of increasingly insecure jobs, we need to understand first how and why things have changed. So let's take a short journey into history to see how we wound up here and why more and more people are sobering up after years of hedonistic consumerism.

A short history of sharing booms

The rapid global expansion of today's sharing economy might seem surprising, but it is not the first time a substantial share of our Western society has shifted from individual to collaborative consumption.

In the late nineteenth century, when many people moved from the countryside to cities in search of work in newly opened factories, town councils began to make vacant public land available to help the poor and hungry collectively grow their own food and improve their living conditions. Community gardens soon became a common sight in Europe, the US and Australia.

During the Second World War, well before the current battles between Uber and taxi drivers, the US government already tried to establish ridesharing as a trend. It encouraged Americans to share spare car seats with others in a national effort to save petrol – a resource needed at the war front. When the oil crisis hit in the 1970s, then-President Carter even introduced a bill to create a National Office of Ridesharing.

There are several examples in recent history where communal living models had a large followership in the Western world. Hippie communes sprang up in the 1960s and 1970s in protest of the Vietnam War. And in 1909 early Jewish immigrants to Palestine started the kibbutz movement of collective living, dreaming of utopian communities inspired by Zionist and socialist principles. The movement dramatically expanded as more settlers arrived in the Promised Land, and in the late 1970s one in 20 Israelis lived in a kibbutz.[8]

However, these recent episodes all have one thing in common: they were linked to a crisis. They appeared during times of economic or political turmoil, when resources were scarce. And they typically faded away soon after.

This is exactly what happened to President Carter's proposal to create a National Office of Ridesharing, which never saw the light of day. Once the oil crisis ended, Americans rekindled their love for driving their own cars. Similarly, community gardens lost their relevance as soon as factory workers started earning enough money to buy food in supermarkets. And Israel's kibbutz movement is facing an uncertain future after an exodus of members.

The pattern seems to be that we gladly share during crises, but quickly return to individualistic overconsumption during recovery. To be sure, community gardens are now experiencing somewhat of a revival among eco-conscious city hipsters, and you can still find the odd hippie tribe on Greek islands or some traditional kibbutzim in Israel. But these early templates of the modern sharing economy never prevailed over the capitalistic cult of private property and consumerism that is at the heart of modern Western economies.

Our long addiction to a throwaway lifestyle

People in the developed world have gotten used to accumulating an astonishing number of things: shoes, clothes, furniture, gifts, toys, sports equipment, kitchen appliances, bric-a-brac. We are surrounded by stuff that we once thought was essential, but that we barely use. We have a habit of junking things soon after we buy them – takeaway coffee cups, plastic bottles, fast fashion.

Deep inside we know that hyperconsumption is unsustainable for our wallets, for our planet and for our souls, yet alternative ways of living have so far struggled to achieve mass appeal. Many of us have become compulsive shoppers, lured by psychologically savvy advertising, unable to resist the urge to indulge in an overabundance of products.

The scary part, says US sociologist Daniel Todd, is that modern consumers are even aware of the mechanisms of modern marketing. We know that our obsession with material goods is as addictive as it is dissatisfying, but we seem unable to change our behaviour. As pop star Lily Allen confesses in one of her songs: "I am a weapon of massive consumption / And it's not my fault, it's how I'm programmed to function."[9]

IN GOODS WE TRUST

The birth of the mass consumption society dates back to the start of industrialisation, but it fully blossomed in the post-war era, when a torrent of consumer goods hit the shelves in the Western world. New production methods increased economies of scale and lowered the cost of manufacturing. Millions of people found work in the growing factory sector.

It was a dramatic change for economies and societies. The industrialisation created new employment, and a mass of new consumers. Life was good: salaries rose and prices declined. So consumers spent more, prompting manufacturers to invest in further expansion, harness further scale advantages, produce more, sell more and create more jobs.

Advertising accelerated the production boom. Billboard, radio and TV commercials raised awareness about new products and sparked desires. Owning a car, washing machine or television became a symbol of social achievement, of status and wealth. People soon viewed collaborative consumption as a phenomenon of pre-boom years, when money was tighter, families were larger, and circles of trust were stronger.

In the old days, if you needed eggs or potatoes, you went to the farmer next door. In the age of supermarkets and mass production, that bond has broken down: consumers today rarely know the person who produces the goods they buy.

The job of advertisers is to restore this bond. Their campaigns aim at making consumers trust a commercial brand as if it was their friend. Slogans and jingles, whether for Coca-Cola or Italian tuna, usually hammer home the same message: Buy me, I won't disappoint you.

Soon enough, the role of marketing expanded from quality reassurance to creating and fuelling needs, calling consumers to action and conveying values well beyond the mere function of a product. Sport shoe producer Nike hires basketball stars to tell us: "Just do it". Cosmetics manufacturer L'Oréal engages Hollywood actresses to say: "Because you're worth it."

And consumers keep buying.

ALL YOU NEED IS LESS

In theory, there's nothing wrong with marketing. People have needs. Companies make goods to meet these needs. Advertisers spread the word. It's a beautiful system. But it is built on the assumption that more goods mean more wealth. It is designed to make factories produce more and consumers buy more.

Already in 1938, an editorial in *Fortune* magazine stated: "The basic and irreversible function of an industrial economy is the making of things; that the more things it makes the bigger will be the income".[10]

Saturation is not an acceptable concept for mass manufacturers, and they avoid slowdowns at any cost. Alfred Sloan, long-time president and CEO of General Motors, understood this earlier than others and came up with a sure-fire method to ratchet up sales: "planned obsolescence".

Sloan realised that consumers would want a new car if they perceived their existing one as old, even if it still worked perfectly well. From the mid-1920s, he made sure the company released new colours and new designs every year, to make car buyers crave the latest model.

The concept quickly spread to other industries, from light bulbs to women's tights. To shorten the cycle and get consumers to replace existing products even more frequently, some designers went so far as to devise goods whose performance diminished over time.

Does the idea of "planned functional obsolescence" seem absurd to you? Check the speed of that smartphone you bought last year and read some articles about the effect of "regular updates" on its battery.

AFTER THE EXCESS THE HANGOVER

"We were poorer, but happier." It's one of those sentences you may have heard before, usually from people older than you. "We didn't have so many things, and we didn't need that much." Apparently, in the good old days, there was less wealth but more happiness. Does that make sense?

It's easy to see how bad our throwaway lifestyle is for the environment. Greenhouse gases are clogging the atmosphere, islands of plastic are drifting in our seas, and rising temperatures are expanding deserts, shrinking water reserves and acidifying the oceans. It's been estimated that if everyone consumed like the average citizen in the Western world, we would need up to four times the earth's resources to sustain the global population.[11] Unfortunately, we only have one planet.

The effect on our souls is less clear. When does having more become too much? How does material wealth affect our wellbeing?

Economists at the University of Oxford found that richer people do feel happier than poorer people, that richer countries tend to have higher average happiness levels and that economic growth boosts happiness over time.[12]

Marilyn Monroe once said it's better to cry in the back seat of a Rolls Royce than on a crowded tram. There's a sad loneliness in this quote that matches an observation of social scientists: people with higher income can afford more – they have access to better healthcare, better schools, better food – but growing material wealth can also be isolating.

The rise of individualistic consumerism, some researchers say, threatens our "social capital", the glue that holds our society together. It weakens our human connection. The most influential expert in the field, Robert Putnam, found that over the past 50 years we have become richer, but more isolated, due to an individualisation of lifestyles.

Brands are successful because our social institutions are failing, says author-activist and consumerism critic Naomi Klein. "We are looking to brands for poetry and for spirituality, because we're not getting those things from our communities or from each other," she told *Fast Company* magazine.[13]

It's a controversial point, and surveys trying to measure the impact of individualistic consumerism on our social lives show mixed results.[14] The concern is real, though. In 2018, the British government appointed the world's first Minister for Loneliness, acknowledging that "for far too many people, loneliness is the sad reality of modern life".[15]

Caught in a vicious cycle of eternal return?

Cyclicality is more than a cornerstone of economic theory. It is a common theme in many world religions, including Hinduism. Philosophers from ancient Egypt and Greece to modern-day thinkers like Friedrich Nietzsche have contemplated theories of "eternal return". According to this idea, the universe and all its energy and all that exists continue to recur an infinite number of times across infinite time or space.

It would mean that every time sequence, good and bad, is set to return for eternity. Nietzsche called it "the heaviest burden": a fate, in which "every pain and every joy and every thought and sigh" forever perpetuates itself without progress, predetermined, unable to improve.[16]

But would this also mean that the cycle of hyperconsumption that was triggered in the past century, if not before, will return time and again? That even the slightest departure from the throwaway lifestyle that has become mentally, environmentally and financially taxing will ultimately prove futile because we're stuck in some weird vicious cycle?

It is the same question that kept Inbal, the Israeli girl in San Francisco, awake that night after dinner: is it worth betting on the continuous growth of the sharing economy?

The answer to Inbal's question may be hidden in a book written three hundred years ago, by a man called Giambattista Vico. A rather unknown yet important thinker from the beautiful and troubled city of Naples in southern Italy, Vico is considered a precursor of the Age of Enlightenment. His thoughts influenced famous philosophers such as Marx and Nietzsche.

What does Inbal have to do with Vico? His masterpiece, *La Scienza Nuova*, can help her (and all of us) predict how history might evolve. It contains two major insights. The first one is that human nature is immutable. According to Vico, men in similar circumstances behave in similar ways, provoking "occurrences and recurrences". This does not imply that the same sequence of events keeps recurring. It just means that life repeatedly asks us to make choices. But humans have a tendency to play out the same pattern of behaviour when faced with similar situations – unless they change the structure of their thoughts.

The theory that men do not intrinsically change, only circumstances do, is not new. Five centuries before

Christ, Greek historian Thucydides reached the same conclusion. Vico's second insight: history doesn't repeat itself in the exact same way because as circumstances change, people can choose to take a different route, and therefore influence the succession of moments.

Vico's theory is revolutionary because he does not conceive history as either a straight line or as a series of circles, irrational in their repetition ad infinitum. He sees humanity moving upward in an ascending spiral – plunging regularly into periods of crisis yet trending towards greater and greater heights. This is why his theory is incredibly modern, and helpful in our times. It enables us to separate human motivations and inclinations (which hardly change) from the social and technological circumstances that evolve across centuries.

Milan Kundera, the Czech author, was equally fascinated with Nietzsche's concept of eternal return, but his conclusion is that nothing is written in stone: "Our lives can stand out against it in all their splendid lightness".

This is our take on centuries of heated debate and thousands of writers' and philosophers' charming words: we move in cycles, but we reach a higher level (and growth curve) all the time.

Nietzsche thought there might not be progress, that history would exactly repeat itself for eternity. But we believe, like Vico, that there is progress. We believe we have reached a new, more advanced level of awareness and consumption.

Why the new sharing economy is here to stay

We are moving in cycles, but we're always evolving. If we can make a prediction, then it's the following: collaborative consumption is here to stay. Why? Because

72

it is economically convenient, logistically efficient, socially enriching and environmentally sustainable.

Toby, Inbal's husband, already saw this coming a few years ago, when he was weighing the pros and cons of switching jobs. In the end, he accepted the new role, trusting in the sharing economy's growth potential. The startup he joined is now one of the world's largest in the ridesharing industry.

The dawn of the third millennium has served the sharing economy a winning hand of three cards: digital technology, economic necessity, and a sobering-up after decades of consumption and production excess. Let's have a closer look at how these factors are contributing to the irresistible rise of collaborative consumption.

THE REVOLUTION OF CLICKS AND SWIPES

Many of Inbal's friends left the kibbutz because they felt constrained in their choices. The goods and income opportunities in their small collaborative community were limited compared to what they could find in the city.

The sharing economy of the kibbutz could simply not compete against the magnified lure of individualistic consumption. Technological progress has changed this premise. The growing mesh of digital sharing platforms is leaving consumers spoilt for choice. These firms offer a similar variety of products and convenience as rivals geared towards capitalistic hyperconsumption.

The modern sharing economy is hugely successful because digital technology has advanced it to a new level of competitiveness. It has filled in once-gaping interstices in the economy. For instance, just a few years ago you couldn't make money driving strangers around in your car. The idea was preposterous. And now you probably know people who do it. Digital technology has made it cheap and easy for consumers to join the sharing game. It has removed important entry hurdles by making deals between strangers trustworthy and efficient.

The trust factor is important. Would you have jumped in a stranger's car twenty years ago? Would you have stayed overnight in a stranger's apartment? Unlikely. Now you do it all the time, encouraged by a myriad of digital ridesharing and home sharing services. Their online feedback and rating systems act both as trustworthiness signals and incentives. They restore the missing bond between seller and buyer in an otherwise anonymous world of products and services.

These apps make every transaction and player transparent. House sharing apps reveal a host's full profile, including comments on how he or she treated previous guests, before you book a bedroom for a stayover. Similarly, you will unlikely leave your host's bathroom in a mess because it could earn you a bad review and reduce your chances of scoring your dream holiday house next summer.

Transaction costs are equally important. Digital sharing platforms are highly efficient in matching buyers and sellers, lenders and borrowers. Their algorithms are fine-tuned to facilitate communication, logistics and payments between two parties without time lags and across continents.

When Inbal's parents wanted to get a lift into town, they had to visit the kibbutz office, write their names on a list and wait for a reply. And remember the old way of renting holiday houses via newspaper ads? It used to be time-consuming to call the owner, negotiate the terms, exchange instructions, transfer money. We used to set up flea market stalls to sell our old vinyl collection and other second-hand stuff. It was a lot of hassle for a few extra bucks.

Online marketplaces offer hassle-free transactions. With the invention of the smartphone in 2007 sharing goods and services has become a matter of clicks and swipes. The smartphone's ability to geo-locate and connect everyone and everything in real time was a game changer. It paved the ground for mass participation in the sharing economy. And that means this time it will be more than a post-crisis flicker.

THE TINDER: CRISIS

When smartphones entered the market, the modern sharing economy was ready to explode. It just needed tinder, and the Global Financial Crisis offered it.

The domino effect from the collapse of Lehman Brothers in 2008 spread well beyond Wall Street. Faced with fatal risks, investors, entrepreneurs and employers all over the world started looking for alternatives to sustain their businesses, their jobs and their lifestyles. The crisis pricked a gigantic real estate bubble and put an end to decades of financial excess, private property cult and an obsession with exclusive ownership. Some sharing apps already existed back then, but it was the financial crisis which spurred people to fully embrace a new way of consuming.

Now it became obvious that many people in the Western world had been living beyond their means for years. Real wage growth had already started to slow in the 1980s, especially compared to GDP and productivity, but household debt continued to mount as central banks lowered interest rates, governments deregulated the financial sector and banks relaxed lending standards. In other words: our income growth was declining yet we continued to upgrade our lifestyle because borrowing was cheap and easy.

Some banks started issuing riskier loans and tried to hide the danger behind sophisticated financial products. When the structure and unsustainability of this game became clear, markets crashed and investment froze. We couldn't borrow money, so we had to start borrowing goods.

Collaborative consumption offered a way out of the financial mess. In 2014, a Nielsen survey showed that cash-strapped Europeans in countries most affected by the crisis were also the most interested in participating in the sharing economy.[17]

Opportunities arose with technology and exploded with need. Businesses flocked into the new sharing market. Hundreds of smartphone apps emerged that encouraged people to earn and save money by sharing cars, summer houses, server capacity and any other asset with "idle capacity".

Those years were full of stories like this one: "On a snowy evening in Paris, Travis Kalanick and Garrett Camp can't get a cab – the idea for Uber is born. The two entrepreneurs found UberCab, a smartphone app that lets people tap a button and get a ride."[18]

A few months earlier in San Francisco, uni friends Brian Chesky and Joe Gebbia had big plans to start a business with their industrial design skills, but had no money to pay their rent.

In a genius act of desperation, they put up some air mattresses in the living room, launched a website to take bookings and turned their apartment into a makeshift "Airbed and Breakfast". It was the start of Airbnb.com, which now offers everything from shared apartments to treehouses.

A wave of new businesses stirred up industries that oligopolies had long ruled, including taxis and transport. This revived price competition. Others offered consumers an opportunity to access expensive assets that were previously reserved for a wealthy elite. A night in a penthouse in Manhattan? Suddenly affordable if you have a sharing app.

Ten years after the crisis, the sharing economy continues to grow. The global economy is in better shape and stock markets in many countries hover around all-time highs.

The law of cycles would imply that, at this point, the sharing economy should falter as consumers return to more exclusive forms of ownership. But market forecasts suggest the opposite. For example, PwC estimates that in Europe alone the sharing economy's most popular areas – collaborative finance, accommodation, transport, and household and professional services – could be twenty times more valuable in 2025, with revenues rising to €570 billion, from €28 billion in 2016.

What is going on? This time the sharing economy is booming right along with an economic recovery instead of being hindered by it, and it keeps spreading. Another storm has passed, but circumstances have changed. Crisis and convenience have changed people's attitudes.

SOBERING UP: THE MINIMALIST MOVEMENT

The sharing economy is outliving the crisis years because we're sobering up after a hyperconsumption orgy that lasted almost one century.

Let's be honest: we've always known about the flaws and contradictions of a highly materialistic lifestyle. We have more stuff, but it makes us lonely. We live longer, but our planet is getting sicker. Yet for decades, we were too complacent to fix things. We've been indulging in a throwaway lifestyle and ignoring its environmental and emotional cost.

We were addicted.

And we would have kept going, perhaps even accelerated, had the global financial crisis not stopped us like a boulder rolling onto a freeway.

The crisis put a brake on our spending binge and forced us to rethink our consumption patterns. We started sharing because we learned that our pockets are not bottomless, no matter how many credit cards we carry. And now that we're at it, we realise that the collaborative lifestyle of reusing, borrowing and sharing goods gives us more than just financial benefits.

In 2015, seven years after the fall of Lehman Brothers, ING bank asked almost 15,000 people in the US, Europe and Australia what influenced their participation in the sharing economy. Most said their strongest motivation was to save money or supplement their income. But a large number of them also said they enjoy collaborative consumption because "it is good for the environment" and "it helps build communities".[19]

You have likely experienced this yourself, when you booked a stranger's apartment on Airbnb because it was cheaper, but you ended up really enjoying your stay because your host's apartment had more personal history, more warmth than a soulless hotel room. When you couldn't find a cab and booked a rideshare, but found that the most memorable part was the encounter with the person driving you around. When you listed old household stuff on eBay to make some money, but realised it made you feel good that your trash was now another person's treasure and didn't end up on the rubbish dump.

Many of the new Mesh businesses openly appeal to a new consumer consciousness. Take New York-based startup *Rent the Runway,* which offers a "rotating wardrobe" of designer clothes for rent on a monthly plan, telling consumers to "shop less". Meanwhile, UK-based furniture-and-art-rental platform Harth encourages consumers to "own less stuff, and surround yourself with things that inspire you."[20] The sharing economy promotes minimalism over excess – and it's minimalism with a rainbow of possibilities.

Our future life as prosumers

The sharing economy is changing more than consumer habits. It is challenging our identity. Much as the gig work trend is blurring the boundaries between employees and business owners, dependent and independent work, we discover that digital sharing platforms let us be several things at once: lenders and borrowers, consumers and producers, tenants and landlords.

The old paradigms are crumbling, and in the future, experts say, we will fuse into a new kind of being: the "prosumer".

Coined by 1980s American futurist Alvin Toffler to describe tech writers of his era, the term "prosumer" now refers to people who aren't just happy to passively buy goods or service. They actively seek to (re)sell them every once in a while or shape them with their own contribution – like a Wikipedia user who refines an article after researching it. Or an apartment's tenant who sublets it on weekly basis while he's away.

We shouldn't fear this trend. We should embrace it.

This convergence of roles can improve our lifestyles, our social interactions and our budgets. The second half of this book will show in detail how pioneers of the Flow Generation are already making the most of the sharing boom to find steady ground in a fast-paced, digitalised world.

For now, let's look at three simple principles that will help us prepare for the future with optimism. Think of them as magic charms to shift from a sense of precariousness to one of possibility.

They state that property is a burden. That any asset (almost) can be monetised. And that you should trust strangers and let them trust you.

PROPERTY IS A BURDEN

It's finally dawning on us: ownership is overrated. The sharing boom is teaching us that we can make do with a lot less than we thought. It's an opportunity to give ourselves a mental x-ray and adjust our lifestyle to our real needs. House prices are rising globally, while wages are stagnating and steady jobs declining. Do we need to own a house? One in five Americans thinks "owning today feels like a burden".[21]

The Flow Generation is changing to new models of collaborative living and home ownership. In densely populated metropoles such as London, San Francisco or Barcelona property investors are converting old warehouses, churches or Victorian townhouses into trendy co-living hubs. They cater for a new generation of highly sociable young professionals, who thrive on personal interaction and are happy to trade privacy for an opportunity to grow their networks.

ANY ASSET (ALMOST) CAN BE MONETISED

The sharing economy is dealing you a win-win opportunity. Today, you can easily milk all sorts of idle assets for cash. Many people still focus on their jobs as the key source of income. The gig and sharing economy are challenging this view. Both allow us to activate an array of income streams from an array of sources. If you own a car, you can make extra money on regular commutes by offering a spare seat to someone going in the same direction.

There are now digital sharing platforms for all sorts of assets: for rooms, for second-hand clothes (such as Thredup in the US), and for hardware tools (such as Borroclub in the UK).

Even less tangible assets are now subject to the sharing frenzy. For example, if you have extra money, you can participate in peer-to-peer lending schemes and get rewarded with above-average interest rates. If you have extra space on your computer drive, you can sign up with a startup called Storj that promises to rent it to others, safely and anonymously.

This is the new reality in the sharing economy. It sparks our imagination in unexpected ways, and the Flow Generation is creatively exploiting the money-making potential of idle assets – by making them available to the crowd.

TRUST STRANGERS AND LET THEM TRUST YOU

Trust is the currency on which collaborative consumption is based, says author and sharing economy expert Rachel Botsman. Winning someone's trust is critical in the sharing economy. It influences the price at which we exchange goods and services, whether it is selling a car or renting a holiday house.

Surveys show that eBay sellers with higher ratings can charge higher prices for the same products than competitors with lower ratings.

Technology is now progressing so fast it has weakened our sense of trust. Many people are wary of the digital platforms, sales chatbots, web apps and social media profiles that are springing up everywhere. We have an in-built fear of cyber criminals, online tricksters and internet imposters who might rob or harm us.

Feedback, ratings and review systems bridge this gap in trust. These systems can turn a collaborative sharing platform into a safer space for transactions than physical marketplaces.

In our future lives as prosumers we will have to learn to use, and trust, these feedback mechanisms more. And it's not just about trusting others. Others also need to trust us. As we participate more frequently in the digital world of collaborative consumption, we are being evaluated by others as much as we evaluate them. We rate Uber drivers and Airbnb hosts and vice versa. Everyone – consumers and producers, tenants and landlords, drivers and riders – is immediately accountable.

A famous ad slogan goes: "You never get a second chance to make a first impression." It's common sense, but in the digital sharing economy our behaviour and reputation weigh double because we are being tracked and it will be increasingly difficult to "clean" or change our virtual profiles and identities.

If you're not paying for it,
you're not the customer.
You're the product being sold.
— Andrew Lewis

Chapter 4

Navigating the data universe:
How to use it without it using you

Halfway up the motorway Vera realised she had made a mistake. Head resting against the seatbelt, she was trying to shake the nauseating jetlag that had gripped her after 24 hours of cabin pressure and airplane food. The chamomile scent of German summer in the car and her dad's booming voice: "Which idiot opened the window?" Vera pressed the automatic closer button. Nothing happened. She pressed again, harder. "Stop it! Stop!! Leave it, for God's sake, it won't lift!" Her dad was furious. "It's the electronics system, this piece of shit. Shouldn't have touched it, dammit."

They drove home with three windows shut and one open, her dad ranting all the way, interrupted only by the pesky friendliness of the voice-controlled navigation system. The digital dashboard was similarly unfazed, still measuring temperature, average fuel consumption, speed. When they reversed into the garage, the display turned into a camera. Through the rear mirror Vera saw her dad on one foot, dangling the other under the bumper to activate the motion sensor that unlocks the boot.

That day she understood that her dad's car isn't a car. It's a computer. A data device that drives.

Trapped in a world of spies

Everything around us is turning into a data device. The things that make our morning coffee, wash our clothes or keep our food cold are now computers disguised as espresso machines, washing machines, fridges. Equipped with touch-screens and timers, they are wirelessly connected to the internet and remote-controlled by our phones, which themselves are pocket computers that can also take photos, show us directions, play music and order food.

Above all, these things record how we live our lives. Every time we use them, we feed others with information about us.

The number of data-tracking sensors worldwide increased sevenfold from around 4 billion to more than 30 billion between 2012 and 2016, according to McKinsey analysts.[1] But connected devices, also known as the "Internet of Things", are just one reason for the sky-rocketing data in our economy. We also leave active trails of personal information whenever we surf the internet, log onto social networks like Facebook, use digital platforms like Airbnb and write emails.

The speed at which we create new data is mind-boggling. Say "one one thousand" in your head. That's about a second. In that time, people worldwide entered almost 70,000 search queries on Google, watched almost 75,000 YouTube videos, published more than 8,000 Tweets on Twitter, made more than 3,000 Skype calls, uploaded almost 900 photos on Instagram and sent more than 2.7 billion emails.[2]

That's how fast the digital universe is expanding in every second. And it keeps growing faster. Not long ago, analysts at leading market research firm IDC found the global data volume was doubling roughly every two years. Now that figure looks too conservative.

It's a veritable data deluge.

"800 PAGES OF MY DEEPEST, DARKEST SECRETS"

Without data masses the gig and sharing economy wouldn't exist. Data is the oil that fuels thousands of startups, from freelance work platforms and e-commerce firms to ridesharing and room-sharing apps.

These firms rely on the insights they gain from sifting through piles and piles of user data. The more data they can get hold of, the more they can refine their services until they are smarter than a genie from an oil lamp. That's the predominant business model in the data-driven gig and sharing economy: to know all your dreams and desires long before you even thought of them, and then to fulfil them on the spot.

Companies in the new platform economy connect the dots between billions of data points, so they can offer each customer the exact product or service he is interested in, anytime and anywhere, and at the highest price he is willing to pay. That's why online shopping platforms like eBay, which track the habits of millions of users, already know what you will likely want to buy next, and for how much. Why a streaming service like Netflix can tell you accurately which movie you will enjoy watching even if you have never heard of it. Why ridesharing platforms like Uber can determine when you will most need a car and gladly pay a higher fare.

Data analytics, the art of making sense of huge data masses, has become big business, worth $166 billion in 2018 and growing fast at almost 12 per cent per year, according to estimates by IDC.[3] The market flourishes on the principle that computers can convert everything we do these days into data and that someone, somewhere can monetise every piece of that data .

Data mining has become so ubiquitous that we have accepted it as a part of modern life. We know that companies track our online browsing behaviour, that supermarkets monitor what's in our shopping carts. We know that tax authorities can look into our bank accounts, that CCTV cameras are filming us in elevators and train stations, and that our smartphones are constantly broadcasting our whereabouts. We know that all the smart things that surround us record more about us than we would probably like.

Still, most of us only have a faint idea of how intrusive the data economy really is. The data spies have no furtive eyes, no lingering shadows, no footprints, and we are blissfully unaware of them monitoring our lives. French journalist Judith Duportail only recently learned, to her surprise, that dating app Tinder had saved every single word she ever entered. "I asked Tinder for my data. It sent me 800 pages of my deepest, darkest secrets", she said in *The Guardian*.

The intimate details that we knowingly or unknowingly share are a treasure trove – and not just for digital platforms and well-known tech giants such as Google and Facebook. Every business, from banks to bookshops, is now in one way or another exploiting digital data to manage its customers and employees. The gig economy with its rising number of freelance, contract and casual workers is intensifying this trend, as we will see later in this chapter. Many employers regularly cooperate with specialised data brokers, firms you may have never heard of like Acxiom or Experian, which bundle and sell personal profiles on millions of people worldwide, pieced together from the virtual trails they leave with every click of the mouse and every touch of a smart device.

We cannot avoid being tracked, no matter how careful we are. Most websites make visitors accept so-called cookies, which allow companies to examine our online behaviour and share the information with third parties, without us having a clue.

In a famous TED talk from 2012, Gary Kovacs, the former chief executive of internet company Mozilla, recalled how he found one morning that not even two bites into breakfast and after visiting only four websites, nearly 25 companies had started tracking him. At the end of the day, 150 sites were collecting his personal information, most of them without his consent. "I look at this picture and it freaks me out," Kovacs told the audience. "I am being stalked across the web."

But the data deluge has two faces, like so many things in the gig and sharing economy. Data analytics can be incredibly convenient if we know how to use it in our favour. Data-driven digital platforms can speed up our chance of finding work, selling stuff, securing credit.

The problem is that the data universe, its players and the strategies they use are evolving so fast that it's hard to keep track of those who are tracking us.

This is the dark side of the gig and sharing economy. We are more exposed than ever before, both as consumers and workers, and this is adding to our sense of precariousness. How do we survive and thrive in a world where it's impossible to draw a clear boundary between private life and business interest? Where everything and everyone, including your health, your love life and your work performance, is tracked by third parties? Are we losing control, or is there a way to tame the data machines?

To cut through the confusion, let's have a detailed look at how data is driving the gig and sharing economy. We need to understand the strategies of digital platforms and how companies use data monitoring to control their increasingly contingent workforces. Let's also take a small step back in history, to the beginning of factory work, to see how we ended up in this modern world of data dominance. Lastly, let's draw some lessons to help us navigate the future as we enter unchartered territory.

Matchmakers: The better marketplace

Data alone is meaningless for a company. If you had a list of the basic physical characteristics of a hundred thousand people, you'd have a giant pile of data, but it would be pretty worthless. You'd want to find the patterns, the relationships. Do short people live longer? Do 60-year-old thin people have stronger hearts than 40-year-old obese ones?

The best-known companies in the gig and sharing economy are successful because they have perfected a system of sifting through vast piles of data to better understand the patterns their customers seek.

Digital platforms – whether they offer work, lodging, or a car seat – are popular because they have proven to be the better marketplaces in our on-demand economy. That's not because of what they do, but how they are doing it. They still sell essentially the same products and services as traditional taxis, hotels or newspaper classifieds, but they operate more efficiently because they have created what economists call "two-sided markets". Digital platforms don't just serve consumers. They serve both buyers and sellers, drivers and passengers, employers and workers, landlords and renters. They are in-betweeners, facilitators.

Two-sided markets make the age-old sales game much more dynamic. In the past, a shop owner would put a product on display and wait for customers to show up. In the on-demand economy there's no more waiting. A digital platform can now help any seller find the perfect match anytime.

It's why Amazon tells you that "customers who bought this item, also bought...". Or why a friend who used a holiday rental app keeps receiving nagging alerts on her phone: "Fancy a spontaneous getaway? Holiday houses are 30 per cent cheaper than average this weekend." The product is now looking for you as much as you are looking for it. Maybe more.

Powerful mathematical formulas enable platforms to make millions of matches every day at the highest price either side is willing to accept at that moment. For each successful match the platform collects a slice of the deal as reward.

For this dynamic pricing model to work, companies need data. A lot of data. From a lot of users.

Airbnb's matchmaking algorithm relentlessly monitors market conditions for subtle changes, says the man who wrote it – a programmer by the name of Dan Hill. The algorithm checks which properties lure the most people in which area at what time. It figures out whether a bedroom sells better if photographed in dim yellow or crisp white light. It calculates the difference it makes, in dollars, if a place is 300 metres away from a river or 3 kilometres.[4]

Hotdog, not hotdog: Who trains the algorithm?

Algorithms can digest a myriad of price signals, as far-fetched as they may seem. But algorithms can only recognise patterns and find meaning in big data if someone trains them. Without human supervision they are dumb and clueless.

There's a funny episode in the US sitcom *Silicon Valley* in which a nerdy programmer shows off his new app "SeeFood" that is supposed to identify food based on snapshots. However, he only taught the algorithm how to recognise a hotdog, and that's as far as its expertise goes. A slice of pizza? A burrito? A shoe?

"Not hotdog," the app proudly proclaims.

Hotdog, not hotdog – an algorithm's understanding of the world is by nature simplistic. Algorithms make decisions based on a toy version of our complex reality and if left unchecked, they can go rogue, applying the same old pattern for eternity. They can act like clueless machines with enormous blind spots, writes US data scientist Cathy O'Neill in her bestseller *Weapons of Math Destruction*. Yet those data-crunching formulas now micro-manage almost every area of the gig and sharing economy.

Algorithms decide whether your personal profile appears on the first page of Google's search results or whether your bank will approve your loan request. They determine how much you pay for an airline ticket or whether your job application gets read.

Most large companies now use computer programs to screen the piles of resumes they receive, and these programs reject up to 75 per cent of CVs before they even reach a human, says London-based career consultant Victoria McLean, who used to work as recruitment manager for two of the world's largest investment banks, Goldman Sachs and Merrill Lynch.

Your income, your health, your livelihood may depend on an algorithm – a formula that may assess you like the hotdog-not-hotdog app and decide, based on an obscure data snapshot of your profile, whether you're in or out. It's a dangerous development because most people are in the dark about the rules that make these programs tick. Companies typically treat algorithms as the "secret sauce" to their business success. Why, when and how they change their models is up to their discretion and can even catch industry insiders by surprise.

This is what happened to Vera's friend Ilana Wechsler, who used to be a search engine optimisation specialist, which means she built websites in a way that they would reliably occupy top ranks in Google's generic search results. But a few years ago, her rankings, and therefore her business, collapsed overnight because Google had secretly updated its algorithm.

"Ranking in Google is a constant cat-and-mouse game," says Ilana. It's a game that pitches humans against algorithms. Ilana decided to get out. Now she specialises in paid web traffic, helping freelancers and other firms post online ads where they will most likely be seen by their target audience.

"It's all about eyeballs," she says. But she adds there's much to gain in this new data-driven world if you know what you're doing.

"You get the ability to slide your business card right under someone's nose at the exact moment they're watching. That's pretty amazing."

Ilana's story holds a lesson: to survive and thrive in the on-demand economy, we need to know how to attract attention. We need to understand the algorithm game if we want to get noticed.

My boss is an algorithm

The data deluge has spilled from consumer markets into our workplaces. Whether we hunt for gigs on a digital platform or still hold a standard job, we face growing pressure to back up our performance with hard data.

Take Katrin, a teacher at a private school in Sydney. Last year, her principal announced a new era of transparency, efficiency and accountability in learning. Computer apps were introduced and a new feedback system established. Katrin and her colleagues learned how to use scorecards and rankings, and new online evaluation modules. She also learned to manage parents who can now – like her principal – track the outcome of every lesson online, so long as Katrin doesn't forget to share the photos and student progress notes she is supposed to take during her classes.

Some days she finds it hard to focus on her teaching because of all the logging on, logging off, rating colleagues, ranking students, giving feedback, collecting feedback, uploading, downloading, digitising, and posting performance results.

"We are all completely overworked just from constantly feeding machines with data," complains Katrin, who says most teachers in her school have grudgingly accepted the obsessive culture of quantifying themselves and others at work as an unavoidable nuisance of life in the digital age.

In fact, they are trying hard to keep up with the new system, knowing that a mediocre performance could cost them their job.

In Australia, teachers are now part of the gig economy. They are the largest contingent worker group. In 2018, almost every second job advertisement (48%) in the Australian education sector offered a temporary, contract or casual role.[5]

While many factors influence the chance of contract renewal, the outcome of a performance review is clearly one of them. Machines are driving it more and more.

In the US, schools already rely heavily on computer-generated performance reviews. But results can be erratic, labelling some teachers as top performers one year and as the worst performers the next, even though they applied exactly the same teaching routine, as Cathy O'Neill describes in her book. Big data software, she says, can come to wild, wacky, and highly unfair conclusions if human beings don't fine-tune it to the ever-changing complexities of our reality.

The data exerts unseen power over your chances to find and keep work in the platform economy.

Platform companies in the logistics and delivery industry make extensive use of data mining and GPS tracking to ensure their service models run at optimum. Their algorithms are potent. They analyse the reviews you leave about ridesharing or food delivery drivers. They track the number of orders their contract workers accept and the money they generate. And they get suspicious if a gig worker declines work too often.

***

An algorithm may fire you and you might never find out why. That's what Tim Monteverde learned, a 19-year-old who just finished high school in Bury, a small English market town near Manchester. In the spring of 2017 he took up a gig as a self-employed Deliveroo rider, on one of the zero-hour contracts that have become a popular casual hiring tool in the British economy. It was work as you go, with no sick pay, holiday pay or employer-paid insurance.

Tim didn't mind. He was so excited he filmed himself on his first official day as bicycle courier, helmet on, smartphone strapped around his wrist. During the long breaks, when no restaurant had food for delivery, he would drop his muddy trekking bike into the dandelions near the creek and play football with the other drivers.

In his best month, after working 12-hour shifts six days a week, Tim earned 2,000 pounds. Until one morning he found himself breathless on the hill behind his house, as Deliveroo's smartphone app refused to sign him on. "Account deactivated. Contact rider support," he remembers reading on the screen.

The support hotline turned out to be a dead end. "Unfortunately, we can only tell you the status of your account. If you want to know why, send an email," he recalls the response of the service staff. Tim wrote one email. Then another one. And another one. He received an automated reply. A promise that his query would be referred. Nothing happened. His account remained shut down.

Tim was locked out of work.

Five weeks and more than a dozen unanswered emails later, he vented his frustration in a YouTube clip.[6]

"It's pathetic," he said.

"You can't just drop someone without even a day's notice and then expecting them to find another job just like this. What if I had to support a wife and three kids and one day my wage and my income are just completely gone? You can't do that to people – just ignoring people after you've gotten rid of them for no reason!"

A year later, Tim is still searching for answers. Did he not generate enough business in his sleepy hometown? Did the he take an unauthorised toilet break? Did this happen because he missed two orders? Was it mere chance that the company moved former colleagues from hourly pay to pay-per-order only days after his app locked him out?

He tried to call the area manager, but the manager had left. And the successor, whom he eventually met, wasn't in the know. Even today, Tim is guessing. A schoolboy sacked by an algorithm.

Questioned about the case, a Deliveroo spokesman told us that every decision at the firm comes from a human, not a machine. He also claimed Tim had not accepted enough orders per hour and had received a warning about the looming account deactivation. Tim, though, maintains he never received any warning or proper explanation.

While it's difficult to know what exactly happened, labour unions are aware of several cases where rider accounts were deactivated overnight with no further explanation.

***

It also matches the experience of Dutch comedian Bardo Ellens, once the Netherlands' most successful YouTube star. In 2006, when he was only 19 and social media still a novelty, his channel *BanjoMovies* had 70,000 viewers. Five years later, his audience had grown to 200,000 people. YouTube elevated him to become a brand ambassador.

Bardo was an influencer, celebrated by newspapers and admired by teenagers. Until one day he searched for his channel in vain. The YouTube algorithm had deleted it with no explanation or warning. Bardo couldn't believe it. "Everything I had done before 2013 – pufff! – gone!" he told documentary filmmakers at Dutch TV VPRO. To this day, he said, he has no clue why the channel was removed, who did it, or why.

"Eight years of work, just gone with a click," said Bardo. "That's how meagre success can be. That's how meagre YouTube can be."

***

Karl Marx, in his observations about the relationship between capital, labour and technology, concluded that machines are simply an instrument in the worker's hand. But in the gig and sharing economy technology is no longer just a simple tool. It has become the boss.

This is another lesson: if you want to survive and thrive in today's world of work, you need to know how to deal with algorithmic bosses who will only listen when they are programmed to.

Even the human bosses must bow to algorithmic demands. When Vera's friend Sam, a regional manager at a façade construction company in Australia, wakes up at 6 o'clock in the morning, the Smartsheet app on his phone automatically spits out two dozen tasks that are due for completion on deadline: sign a contract, review the progress of people in his team, finish a draft plan to avoid project delays. Failure to complete these tasks threatens Sam's personal performance targets – and job outlook. "It's huge pressure to perform," he says.

Still, as a society we have developed unconditional faith in the power of data-crunching machines at work. Data, the common narrative goes, is objective. It allows us to make purely factual, "evidence-based" decisions free from emotions and personal biases. That's why the use of data analytics, algorithms, machine learning and electronic performance management is spreading across our workplaces.

We have come to trust computers more than ourselves. Just look at Facebook whose algorithms have become so efficient at tracking our likes, preferences and habits that, according to researchers at Stanford University and the University of Cambridge, they can make more accurate judgments about our personalities than even our closest friends.[7]

A brief history of the stopwatch society

The desire to quantify and monitor people at work is nothing new. It goes back to the dawn of mass production when Frederick Taylor, foreman in a steel company in Pennsylvania, laid the groundwork for modern performance management.

Like many people at the time, Taylor was convinced that simple factory labourers lacked the brains to understand how to do their jobs properly and needed an intelligent manager to tell them. Taylor spent long hours trying to figure out rules every manager could use to organise labourers and get more work done in less time. His underlying logic: you can only improve what you can measure.

Armed with a stopwatch, Taylor began to monitor a steelworker's every move. He timed how long it took a man to lift a piece of iron from the furnace, carry it up a plank and drop it on a railroad car. He then mapped out the ideal work pattern – when to stop, when to turn, when to take a break, when to drink some water – until the workers he observed were able to carry four times as much iron in a day. In 1911, he published his *Principles of Scientific Management* in a thin book.

Taylor's principles, known as Taylorism, were highly influential in the early years of mass production. They suited workplaces like Ford's car factories where labourers performed the same mechanical tasks over and over again.

But the system was flawed. It was based on the notion that humans are made for endless hours of monotonous work routine. Labour unions began to question the impact of Taylorism. After the Second World War new management approaches took hold. Toyota's car factories made headlines because they granted even simple labourers a high degree of independence in making decisions and solving problems in small teams.

The rise in white-collar work further eroded Taylor's assumption that workers were most efficient in robotic procedures. Instead, corporate leaders began to recognise that they achieved more if they focused on managing people, not processes. They asked: how do we enhance the performance of creative knowledge workers in office cubicles?

Peter Drucker, the most progressive American management consultant of the 20th century, led the way. He advocated for a flexible, collaborative workplace, in which managers are happy to delegate power and – much like coaches – motivate employees to give their best. Employees in turn are willing to work hard because they believe in a company's mission, values and goals.

Rapidly expanding online markets and increasingly fickle customers have pushed managers to the edge. They realised that they need speed and agility to survive in the era of e-commerce and e-business.

In 2001, a group of software developers met in a ski resort in Utah and coined a new, anarchic style of getting work done, known as "agile management". Their mantra: topple corporate bureaucracy, build small teams of motivated individuals, give them the environment and support they need, and trust that they will reach a target in whichever way they think is best.

Agile management is a buzzword of the on-demand economy. It has put performance management into the hands of the worker.

The agility trend explains why companies are now happy to meet client needs by scrambling together highly autonomous project teams of freelancers and full-time staff. It explains the new culture of boardroom walls littered with fluoro stickie notes and daily check-in meetings held standing to save time.

In the on-demand economy everything is always moving, always in flow. Agile management seems like a natural fit for our fluid times. It values responding to change more than following a plan.[8]

FREE(LANCE), BUT ALWAYS TRACKABLE

The new workplace autonomy in the on-demand economy has a price: privacy. As freelancers, contractors or gig workers we are expected to be flexible, agile, ready to fulfil rapidly changing client needs. We can work from anywhere, yet we're always trackable.

In a modern twist on Taylorism, companies are rediscovering the value of meticulously measuring, tracking and monitoring workers. Only today, they use high-tech gadgets from the Internet of Things to collect data and optimise a worker's performance, not simple stopwatches like Taylor did.

We're trackable in startling ways. In the mining industry, hard hats with mounted sensors measure a remote worker's brain waves for signs of fatigue.[9]

Mobile beacons record the step patterns of warehouse workers and digital wristbands track their heartrate.[10] E-commerce giant Amazon, already under scrutiny for enforcing a high-performance, high-surveillance work culture, recently confirmed it patented a high-tech bracelet that can monitor whether warehouse workers are putting their hands in the right places.[11] Call centres commonly use voice analysis software that records the tone of customer service representatives and nudges them to sound friendlier on the phone.[12]

GPS tracking is rife across the economy, including among delivery and ridesharing drivers. Surveys by time-tracking software provider TSheets revealed that in 2017 one in three employees in the United Kingdom, in the US and in Australia were exposed to GPS tracking at work.[13] In the UK, one in five respondents said they were being tracked 24 hours a day, which would be illegal. As many as one in four employees in Canada said they could not switch their GPS tracking device off.

Mobile software with names such as Clockshark can track, for example, whether construction workers are on site or having a toilet break. Freelancers who sign up on Upwork typically agree to have computer screenshots taken every 10 minutes to reassure clients they're doing their job.[14]

Employers have become reliant on tracking software and data-collecting devices to manage the performance of an increasingly dispersed workforce of contractors and freelancers – people who are always on the move, always all over the place. Researchers at the University of London found that wearable devices can boost a worker's productivity by 8.5 percent.[15]

But the explosion of data-tracking devices also allows management to collect more information than ever before about workers, in ways hardly imagined during Taylor's lifetime, warns Phoebe Moore, a political economist at the University of Leicester. Her book *The Quantified Self at Work in Precarity* gives an unsettling account of how the data deluge is blurring the boundaries between work and private life, between performance management and plain surveillance. Moore recounts a yearlong trial of a Dutch company she was invited to observe as a researcher. The company handed out 30 Fitbit wristbands in what was initially seen as a welcome test run to improve the health and wellbeing of employees.

Fitbits can count steps, measure heart rates, stress levels, calories burnt and sleep patterns, and they're popular among sports and fitness enthusiasts. Their use at work is more controversial, as the Dutch experiment shows. Once the initial enthusiasm waned, participants began to question what their employer would do with all the deeply personal data. In the end 75 per cent had dropped out.

A company can find out more about us than we could ever have imagined, and this is adding to the sinking feeling that our lives are getting more precarious. The data trails we leave everywhere, consciously or unconsciously, can end up in our employer's hands and allow them to make conclusions about our performance. What if your fridge told your employer that you're having more than the recommended amount of alcohol per week? What if the corporate wellness app, based on keywords in your search history, suspected you were pregnant and told your employer before you could even tell your partner?

Or what if a monitoring device blurted out your secrets to the world? An American couple had a disturbing experience with Amazon's smart home device Echo. The machine's virtual assistant Alexa silently recorded a private conversation between the couple and shared it with one of the husband's employees. Amazon, in a media statement, said the device had misinterpreted several words in the background conversation as commands in what the firm called an "unlikely" string of events.[16]

Lawyers at Privacy International, an NGO fighting for data privacy, warn that companies can train their algorithms to look for specific keywords in social media chats to make assumptions about your trustworthiness, your reliability, your creditworthiness. Common phrases, such as "I'm running late", used too often in a chat, could earn you an entry as "unreliable" in some databank somewhere in the world. It could bar you from getting hired, from getting bank credit, from getting a cheaper health insurance deal.

How companies use data profiling to let computers make automated decisions remains highly opaque.

"It's creepy if it's inaccurate, but it's equally creepy if it's accurate," says Ailidh Callander, a London-based lawyer at Privacy International.

If that makes you uneasy, just look at China where officials have started rolling out a new "social credit system" that monitors and rates the behaviour of every citizen for sincerity and trustworthiness: what they buy in shops, what they post on social media, whether they pay their telephone bill on time.

Rachel Botsman, author of *Who Can You Trust?*, calls it a futuristic version of "Big Data meets Big Brother", a nightmarish people surveillance system based on unfairly reductive algorithms that produce trust scores without considering the context.[17]

Scared of the future? Let's turn the tables!

We are living in the data age and it's pointless to try to turn back time. Sure, we can continue to complain about the data deluge, get upset every time the media exposes a new scandal – be it Cambridge Analytica's misuse of Facebook data or the British public health service's illegal sharing of the personal data of millions of patients with a Google-owned company, with the pharma industry and with insurance firms.[18]

The public outcry that usually follows such high-profile data breaches is healthy and has already gotten politicians thinking. The European Union just reformed its rules to give people more control over their data and create a "level playing field" between consumers and businesses.[19]

Institutions will eventually catch up with the data explosion around us. Governments will continue to strengthen data privacy laws. But it might take years for them to effectively rein in corporate data exploitation. In the meantime, we will have to do more than just freak out about underhanded deals and eavesdropping devices.

There are two strategies to reclaim our power as consumers and workers: defence against data sharing and fighting back to make big data work for us, not against us. We can use both at the same time.

DEFENCE: THE INTERNET DIET

The first step to shoring up our defences is uprooting the spies. You probably can't fend off all the data-tracking cookies that follow us on the internet, but there are plenty of tutorials and apps that help consumers restore their online privacy.

You don't need to be a tech geek to disable cookies on your computer, switch on the ad blocker and use your browser's incognito window to surf the web without leaving a data trail. Add-on programs such as Firefox Lightbeam or Ugly Email can reveal which companies are tracking you on the web or reading your emails. Several providers, including Signal, offer encrypted messenger services.

For a more radical move, you can go on a social media diet. While this may not be for everyone, millions of people around the world are questioning the benefits of online networks due to growing concerns over unauthorised data harvesting. When marketing consultancy Edelman asked 9,000 people worldwide in 2018 whether social media platforms behave responsibly with user data, 60 per cent said no. Only one in four respondents in France, Germany and the UK said they trust social media.[20] In another poll, half of all social media users in Germany said they are considering deleting their social media accounts.[21]

Facebook's image in particular has suffered heavily following the Cambridge Analytica scandal, in which the social network leaked data of as many as 87 million users to the political consultancy that worked for the Trump election campaign. In mid-2018, Facebook reported for the first time in its corporate history that it lost millions of active users in Europe.[22] User numbers in the US and Canada have so far held up, but in a large poll by the Reuters Institute across 40 countries respondents labelled the social network as a "creepy, ego-centric, uncool uncle".

The growing public pressure led Facebook to overhaul its privacy policy and cut ties with several large data brokers earlier in 2018. While the changes may not be as far-reaching as some may want, they still show the power consumers have over a brand.

If enough people refuse to play the data game by the rules of big tech, companies will feel the heat and listen. However, there are trade-offs. Quitting all social media isn't helpful if you want to succeed in the gig and sharing economy. Social networks can be immensely powerful, low-cost tools to quickly spread a message, to market yourself and to attract the attention of potential employers and clients – a method known among digital marketers as "growth hacking". Similarly, banning all sorts of smart devices from your home may neither be practicable nor desirable.

It's all about the perspective. People can consciously use internet-connected devices to save money. For example, health and life insurers are piloting programs that offer preferential rates and discounts to customers who agree to have their health monitored with a Fitbit bracelet. Car insurers are experimenting with black boxes and other so-called telematics tools that track and reward good drivers with lower premiums.

It all depends. The watchdog can chase away friends. We better train it.

FIGHTING BACK: THE DATA COUNTERATTACK

If we want to resist companies that harvest our personal data, we may feel like David battling Goliath. But we have more power than we think, as consumers and as workers. We should dare to use it.

In London, the small but vocal Independent Workers' Union of Great Britain (IWGB) shows how to turn the tables in this data-driven on-demand economy. Most of its members are migrants. Many are gig workers: cleaners, couriers, ridesharing drivers. Many are notoriously underpaid, says IWGB press officer Emiliano Mellino. They signed zero-hour contracts or became "independent contractors" because they had no other choice. And while many of the union's members enjoy the flexibility and freedom of working on their own terms, they also know that they are probably the weakest link in a battle against machines and data dominance at work.

Mellino, a former finance reporter for Reuters, is a patient listener and a passionate speaker. The union's gig workers confide in him, share their experiences and fears. He recalls the story of a delivery driver who was shocked to find out that his employer even tracked the battery level of his mobile phone.

"What else do they know? Why can they get away with this?" workers ask him, and Mellino replies that companies have become complacent because few workers challenge them.

The IGWB routinely brings employers before court for breaching the law, but it's a long and cumbersome process that can drag out over a year, says Mellino. His union has learned to wield a more powerful weapon: making noise. A lot of noise. In public. While the lawyers joust at high levels, Mellino and other union members attack from the grassroots.

Armed with samba drums, megaphones and whistles, they recently stormed the headquarters of consulting firm Ernst & Young in a flash protest against threatened layoffs and work hour cuts among its outsourced cleaners. Stunned by the sudden brouhaha in the glass-clad foyer, security staff sounded the fire alarm and ordered the immediate evacuation of the building.

"Imagine that," says Mellino. "They think you're not going to fight back. But if 40 people with whistles and drums are able to shut down Ernst & Young's entire headquarters for hours, imagine what you can do."

Shortly after the protest, Ernst & Young's outsourcing company cancelled the planned cuts.

***

Trying to fight back all by yourself is a lonely and rather hopeless mission. But join a collective and your power will skyrocket. Legal experts say there is ultimately only one way to rebalance the massive asymmetry of power in our data-driven economy: tightening the laws and making sure companies comply. In other words, institutions must change and authorities must show their teeth.

What can we do as individuals – as workers, consumers, citizens? We can keep up the political pressure by supporting lawmakers who campaign for stronger consumer protection and data privacy rules. Politicians in several countries, including the UK and Germany, are also debating whether to hit tech giants with a "big data tax" or "digital services tax". [23]

The thinking behind this push: why treat data any differently from car parts? If a company makes money with the data consumers provide for free, wouldn't it be only fair for governments to tax the company's profit and funnel some of the money back to consumers? These are not questions we want to answer for you, but they are definitely worth asking in the next electoral campaign.

Most of us have gotten into the habit of giving away our personal data for next to nothing. A few years ago, a Canadian software engineer by the name of Andrew Lewis made a statement somewhere on the internet that was so catchy it went viral: "If you're not paying for it, you're not the customer. You're the product being sold."

It's a simple truth that defines nearly every service we use on the internet these days. Instagram, Facebook, Dropbox, WhatsApp, Twitter, LinkedIn, Pinterest, TripAdvisor – it's all for free, except that it's not. As users we pay with an invisible currency: our personal information. Every post we like, every article we share, every photo we upload, every comment, rating and review we leave on these pages is worth money. How much money exactly? Well, that's less clear.

Internet companies typically say users are adequately reimbursed for the data they provide because they receive a free service in return that gets better all the time, as machines learn to understand what users like and dislike. On the most basic level, the argument seems to make sense. Take Facebook, for example. The company's official records show that it earned on average around US$8.80 of revenue for each user in Europe and almost US$26 for each user in North America during the first three months of 2018.[24] If we think of this amount as the value of our personal data, it might seem like a fair deal to get a free service in exchange.

However, several experts point out that our personal data is worth a lot more than the official figures suggest. This is because our data is constantly sold, bought and traded among multiple companies. But as consumers we have no control over where our data ends up and at what price.

The rule of thumb is that the more details we share, the more valuable our data becomes, ranging from a few cents to several hundred dollars per person.[25] Hong-Kong based data startup Datum estimates that a person's full profile, one that includes health and location data, is worth more than US$2,000 (find out how much your own digital trail is worth: https://calc.datum.org).

In their provocative new book *Radical Markets*, American economists Eric Posner and Glen Weyl argue that data should not be treated as a company's capital, but as a form of labour.[26] In their view, consumers deserve more than just a free social media service full of ads in return for the data masses they provide without charge and usually without awareness.

So, what if you could just hire someone as your bounty hunter? Someone who is equally annoyed that big companies are making big bucks with our deepest personal secrets, while we stay behind empty-handed.

A bunch of startups has begun to figure it out. They are scattered across the globe, from Hong Kong to Amsterdam, but unified in their mission to help consumers reclaim control and a slice of the profit that tech giants earn with human data.

Most use modern blockchain technology to build digital marketplaces where people can store and sell their personal data on their own terms. People sign up on the platform, which then hunts for companies who are interested in accessing the collective's personal data in exchange for cash or cryptocurrencies.

The big vision: instead of logging into Facebook, people would just sign into their personal data marketplace of choice. There, they would keep the lid on every piece of personal information – or lift it for businesses who pay a reward.

London-based CitizenMe calls it "a democracy in its truest sense". However, many of these startups are still in their infancy and struggling to achieve scale. New-York based Datacoup, for example, initially paid several dollars in data-sharing rewards to its members until it ran out of funds. Datum, based in Hong Kong, says it attracted more than 20 advertisers and companies who purchased $150,000 worth of data from the 60,000 users on its platform.

It might take years until these firms – with names like Wibson, Data Republic, Meeco, Ocean Protocol and Iota – are mass-market ready. But there is a good chance that at least a few of them will forever change the way tech companies treat our personal information.

We are witnessing the beginning of a data revolution from the grassroots level. The new business models could redraw the line between data use and data exploitation and help us reclaim our bargaining power. Data exchanges offer one way out of the perceived precariousness in the gig and sharing economy because they put the people back in control. And they offer a secondary income source at a time when permanent, secure jobs are in decline.

"The asset is already there," says Matt Hogan, Datacoup's founder. "If a firm comes up to you and says: we treat your data as an asset and help you monetise it, why wouldn't you do it? It opens up another revenue stream."

Paid online surveys, which can be completed on websites such as Swagbucks, Toluna or i-Say.com, may be another way to trade personal data in exchange for money. Unfortunately, they can be highly frustrating, as British writer Joe Bish found out. He spent a whole day doing online surveys to see if they can actually make you any money and ended up with nothing but an e-voucher from a company called My Photobook.

"Turns out eight hours of sitting and clicking little bubbles isn't an easy way to riches," he wrote in an online article.[27]

Part II

How do we stay afloat?

O ur economies are changing faster and in more ways than we can imagine, and the unpredictability is pushing us out of our comfort zone. Stable jobs are turning into insecure gigs. Our incomes are increasingly uncertain, as we're speeding into a future where the majority of us will work on our own account – as freelancers, short-term contractors or perhaps world-roaming part-timers. We have to learn to manage ourselves and our algorithmic bosses. And we must reassess our real needs after decades of addictive hyperconsumption have left us feeling numb atop a pile of household debt.

These are testing times because the exponential growth of the gig, sharing and data economies is radically challenging old patterns, concepts and values. Wherever we look, the boundaries are blurring between humans and machines, between mine and yours, between precarity and stability, between feeling vulnerable and stepping into our power. Our existence is increasingly fluid. Career paths we used to take for granted are crumbling. Diplomas we used to associate with success are looking more like just parchment. Safety nets we expected to protect us are growing holes. We even question our identity because today everyone can be several things at once: employee and business owner, landlord and tenant, consumer and producer.

The current wave of disruption is tremendous and unstoppable. Still, we have every reason to believe that institutions will eventually catch up, as they have in previous waves of technological progress. Robots will destroy some jobs, but technology will create new ones. Labour laws will change. Governments will intensify their efforts to sanction rogue employers and protect the most vulnerable workers. Some internet companies have begun to shore up their users' data privacy protections.

People are powerful. We have a voice to criticise developments that go too far.

We all shape the world we live in as much as the world shapes us, so long as we stop resisting change. This is what Adrián, Alessandro, Lachlan and Vera learned in the months and years after they found themselves at crossroads in their lives.

Most of them would have preferred to continue on a path that their parents' generation would have described as sturdy: a full-time corporate job, a formal education, and a living space they could call their own. But they also realised that the world has moved on and that the old way of doing things is not serving them anymore.

***

ADRIÁN. MADRID. FINDING A HIDDEN TALENT.

Silence. Why is no one answering his question? If Adrián was to film his worst nightmare, this might be the opening scene: him alone in a room full of eyes silently staring back. His hands are getting sweaty, but maybe it is the heat from the overhead projector, the beam of light burning on his forehead. "This is not my place," he thinks.

Adrián feels safe behind the camera or his computer screen, sunk deep into the world of pixels and movie making. He remembers the last botched attempt to change careers, when he was so desperate for money he tried his luck as a phone dispatcher at Corte Inglés, the Spanish department store. It was his best-paying job so far, 600 euros a month, but he couldn't get used to the non-stop talking and soon returned to his old life as a creative introvert.

"I don't know what else to do. I don't know how to do anything else," he kept telling himself. He was stuck. It never occurred to Adrián that he'd have what it takes to be a lecturer. He couldn't believe it when a friend got in touch one day, completely out of the blue, to mention a vacancy at a local university in Madrid. "You'd be the right man," the friend said. "It's audiovisual communication and it's urgent."

Had his friend seen a talent he had yet to discover in himself? Now, two lessons into his part-time teaching gig Adrián breaks the silence. He walks out of the projector's beam and meets the eyes of his students. "Listen, I know exactly how you feel," he says. "I used to be the shyest kid in class. But look where I am now. I'm standing here as a teacher, and I'm telling you that you can achieve anything you want. So, let's work together."

It's a watershed moment for Adrián. Students meet him after class and open up to him. Some share their worries with him. Others tell him they're thrilled to finally learn from an academic with real-life industry experience, someone who has actually worked on a movie set.

For the first time in six years, Adrián feels truly appreciated as a professional. It boosts his confidence. And something else happens this month that Adrián finds miraculous: three clients in a row book him for video projects via a digital work platform, the most since he started his freelance career last year.

ALESSANDRO. AMSTERDAM. OVERCOMING DOUBT.

Some bring their wives, ready to impress. Alessandro zips up their wetsuits, clips them into the harness and leans with them against the wind during a dry run on the beach before he sends them off into the grey chop of the Ijsselmeer.

Kitesurfing has this adrenaline factor that gets you hooked. Although not everyone does. There are the loud ones, all pumped and smiles and thumbs up on the day, but they never return. And then there are others, the clumsy ones with no obvious talent and no sense of balance, who keep coming back week after week. Until they have figured out how to merge their bodies with the power of the kite and fly.

What makes some unlikely people succeed and others not? Alessandro has been thinking a lot about this in the years since leaving the corporate law firm in Brisbane. First living off his savings, then working as a kitesurf instructor in Cape Town, before following his Dutch girlfriend to Amsterdam.

Somewhere along the way he sets up his profile on freelance work platform Upwork as a legal consultant, and when a startup from the United States emails him to see if he can give urgent advice on blockchain technology, Alessandro jumps at the opportunity. He's fascinated by blockchain and has read a fair bit, but lacks deep experience in this space.

What does that make him? More amateur than expert? Bold?

Afraid of overselling himself, Alessandro decides to give an honest yet confident reply. He doesn't want to pass on a project that could kickstart his freelance career, a career working online from anywhere in the world. "Okay," he tells the client. "I still don't know every detail, but I believe in your project and I'm willing to learn on the go." He gets three weeks to deliver.

Alessandro works frantically, often late into the night, until he is familiar with all the legal intricacies of the project. And when the job is done – he really, truly pulled it off – he changes his online profile: "Alessandro Mazzi – legal consultant for tech startups and blockchain projects."

This is my niche, he convinces himself. By now, success seems more likely than failure to Alessandro, a corporate dropout trying to juggle a gig as casual kitesurf instructor and an uncertain future as a freelance online legal consultant. Friends doubt him. He has doubts, too, but he tries not to overthink.

All these weekends spent in wetsuits on the beaches outside Cape Town and Amsterdam had taught Alessandro why his least talented students could succeed and why he can too: he is fiercely determined.

LACHLAN. SINGAPORE. LEARNING BY DOING.

He calls it "carpet bombing": dropping so many business cards in one location that his name spreads like wildfire across the condominiums with their immaculate interiors and well-clipped lawns and palm-lined lap pools. Here, restless expat wives take a plunge before breakfast and at night their wealthy husbands, bankers and managers, return from the nearby business district to wash off Singapore's tropical heat.

Lachlan places a stack of promotional cards on the gym's reception desk. If he can get four or five clients per day in one condo, he's sorted. Better than zigzagging around the city all day. And he likes the expats, not just because they are a breeze to work with and pay the full rate even if they cancel a workout last minute as can happen, cashed-up and time-poor as they are. Some of them have genuinely become friends.

It's been a year since he left Spain. His dad got a job offer in Singapore, and Lachlan decided to follow. He had already figured out in Valencia how to run a business and target the right clientele in the aftermath of the financial crisis, when none of the locals had money to spare and expats were rushing out of the country in droves. He was a certified personal trainer with no savings, no high school certificate, no brand and no training studio. But he had the beach, his charm and a nothing-to-lose attitude.

"Lucky" was his nickname, but for Lachlan things never simply fell into place. In Singapore he worked hard for luck to strike, using his curiosity and passion for psychology to think from his client's mind and offer a product that met demand. It was learning by doing. A crash course in marketing, taught by reality. And if that sounds straightforward, it wasn't.

From the moment he got locked out of school, Lachlan's education has been an exercise in trial and error. He picks up martial arts and improves so fast that his hobby turns into a serious side business.

People pay to see him in professional tournaments across Asia.[1] It gives him the confidence to continue honing his skills on his own. Lachlan knows he can succeed.

Buzzing with ideas, he keeps exploring. He gets up before sunrise to study business strategy, app development and startup management. He enrols in online seminars on marketing and branding, reads e-books, watches YouTube tutorials. Lachlan follows his interests and becomes an opportunity hunter.

Once, he hires four specialists in Bulgaria to help him design smartphone apps. He launches a watch brand with a friend and gives it the London luxury look and feel. Instagram models start wearing his timepieces on bare skin, earning him thousands of followers – a testament to his ability to dive headfirst into a new venture and unlock markets for himself. Today, 25-year old Lachlan is an expert in social media marketing.

There are setbacks. A coding course turns into a money dump when, a couple of weeks after enrolling, Apple shifts to a new coding language. It renders useless everything Lachlan has learnt about coding.

That's the world of education as he knows it: in the fast-moving digital space, you can't sit still or your skills get left behind. "It's Darwinism at its finest," says Lachlan. "You either adapt or you die."

VERA. SYDNEY. LIFE IN THE HAPPY HOUSE.

"So, have you lived with children before?" The guy who came to see the spare room is shuffling nervously on his chair. He is tall and skinny, wears dreadlocks and sneakers and talks in an Eastern European accent about his studies in graphic design.

He watches the toddler bounce up and down on Vera's lap. "No, uhm, not really," says the guy. He is in his twenties and desperate to move out of a hostel, where he shares a twin bedroom with a backpacker. "Life with children is... uhm... new to me. But I'm happy to give it a try."

He's in. Vera smiles. "Don't worry, it's also new to us," she says.

Interviews like this one have become a regular part of the house share and Vera feels she is living in a social experiment: How long can we do this for? How long can a young family hold on to a piece of urban paradise – a large house with a subtropical garden in one of Sydney's most expensive beach suburbs – and still pay only one bedroom's worth of rent in exchange for some reinvented communal living model?

"I'm not moving anywhere until the landlord throws us out," says her partner Lars.

It will take another decade before the landlord does decide to sell the property and cancel the lease. By then, the share house will have lodged more than two dozen housemates and hosted hundreds of guests. And it will have seen two children grow up, whose favourite get-to-know-you game will be to drag new housemates to the big globe that sits on the chest of drawers in the surfboard room and get them to point out their hometown.

They meet students and working professionals from all over the world. There's a marine biologist from Tahiti and a German-speaking Italian from Ethiopia, an Australian astrologer and a French-Canadian with a love of sports cars. There's a band manager from India, a devout Catholic architect and a gay social worker from England. Most of them are surfers. And many, often to their own surprise, stay for years. Max, a French-Tahitian filmmaker, stays for eight. He becomes the backbone of the co-living community.

"Our happy house", he calls it.

How do we stay afloat?

There's something comforting, say those who live there, in finding a home away from home. A place in between student hostel and hippie commune, where you can spend gin-and-tonic nights with your friends at the wooden garden table near the rosemary bush and the clothes line full of kids' socks, and wake up hungover to the smell of spaghetti Bolognese for Sunday lunch.

***

Adrián, Alessandro, Lachlan and Vera are pioneers of the Flow Generation: agile, opportunistic and adaptable. Confronted with themselves and the endless, bewildering changes of our times, these young people learned how to navigate the liquid life. They discovered hidden talents and unexpected opportunities to make and save money. Faced with a world in which technology is fast dissolving old beliefs about right or wrong moves, they also lost their fear of failure.

They have embraced what Heraclitus taught already thousands of years ago. This universe is built on contrast. All that is around us and within us exists in a balance of opposites. There's never challenge alone; there must be opportunity in equal parts. So, while the big shifts that come with the rise of the gig, sharing and data economies fuel a growing sense of insecurity, they also beckon.

Precisely because digital technology is now so available and affordable, the hurdles to taking fate into your hands and being successful are lower than ever. The tales of Adrián, Alessandro, Lachlan and Vera show that bold moves and a trial-and-error attitude can get you further than ever these days because digital technology acts as a catalyst. New startups are emerging, online social networks and communities are spreading fast and far, alternative models of working, learning and saving for the future are gaining traction.

Let's find out in the next four chapters what this means in practice and how it is possible these days to have a career, a relevant education, a safety net and a home, at a time where traditional institutions are crumbling and shifting labour markets are forcing more and more people to rely on themselves.

I am not what happened to me,
I am what I choose to become.
— Carl Jung

Chapter 5

Work:

From nine-to-fivers to job jugglers

The rapid rise of the gig economy has thrown the Western world into an identity crisis. Within only a few years, our once-solid work routine has cracked and crumbled. Now we're sliding into a future in which the standard full-time job with all its perks and stability will likely be the privilege of a minority.

We watch with fear and awe how quickly artificial intelligence and digital technology are taking the helm at our workplaces. It's a classic case of NIMBY (Not In My Backyard) thinking: we love digital innovation – as long as it doesn't get too near our job security.

The problem is that we can't pick and choose. Digital technology is dramatically changing our lives and there's no escaping the fact that more, if not most, of us will rely less on traditional corporate work structures in coming years.

Two fears are tied to this prospect. The first is financial. Digital platforms are emerging as the new marketplaces for work and they seem to be dealing out gigs like traders at a topsy-turvy Dutch auction where the lowest bidder wins. "The internet is enabling a new kind of poorly paid hell," warns US magazine *The Atlantic*. The article speaks to a gut unease about our future. How are we supposed to make money in a globalised gig economy that pits freelancers from all over the world against each other?

The second involves identity. Many people today equate occupation with vocation. They strive for a career that gives them meaning, fulfilment and purpose. Work is a natural extension of their personality.

Who are we without a proper job to our name?

Hundreds of years ago, people belonged to a place or a clan. Their names reflected it. Wanderers whose paths would cross in the Swedish plains or Austrian mountains would immediately recognise their ties when hearing each other's last name. "I'm Svensson" (Sven's son), they might say, or "I'm the Eder," signalling that they come from an arid area (Eder being a derivation of *oede*, meaning barren).

In less developed corners of the world, you still identify with a tribe. You belong to people. Travel to the South Pacific and the icebreaker question is: "Who do you know?"

In the developed world, however, we moved on, and our last names began to reflect our occupations. We became a "Smith" or "Baker". We became our jobs.

Think about the last time you met a stranger. After how many minutes did one of you ask: "What do you do?" And didn't the answer ("I'm an investment banker", "I'm a plumber") allow for endless assumptions about the other? We are used to putting people in boxes based on the job they do.

Job jugglers

The gig and sharing economies undermine this kind of thinking. Labour markets are changing so fast, and there are now so many different ways to earn income that our overidentification with one occupation just ignores reality. Vera's parents worked as teachers from when they finished university until they left the workforce as pensioners. That's almost half a century spent doing the same job. Nicoló's parents have been working as doctors for as long as they can remember.

For the Flow Generation, the days of a professional identity for life are over. Careers don't fit into neat boxes anymore. Vera's 8-year-old daughter dreams of becoming an ice-cream van driver, an artist, a shopkeeper and an architect. Everything at once. And there's a real chance she will be all these things at some point in the future: part-time architect and freelance artist with an Etsy online shop and a side hustle selling ice cream on the local market.

Millions of people around the Western world have already become job jugglers. They lead a patchwork existence, stitched together by several occupations, gigs and passive income sources. Technology is fostering such fragmented working lives, and it changes the premise of how we think about ourselves.

The challenge is huge because it affects everyone, but not everyone is prepared for a world without linear career paths and strong workplace institutions that secure us emotionally and financially. Digital technology is breaking up our solid work identity and flinging us into uncertainty.

It shifts the core question from "What do you do?" to "What are you good at?"

Once you can answer this question, the future will be brighter than you may think.

Companies still need skilled, inspired people to make and sell their products and services. And they are willing to pay the price for them. Consultancy Willis Towers Watson recently asked 900 companies in 38 countries how automation and digital technology will influence their hiring. Around two-thirds said they expect to employ talents more flexibly and remotely by 2020. Sixty-two per cent anticipate paying more for people who have the specific skills they need.[1]

Work is not disappearing. It is changing. Old jobs are giving way to new jobs. New technology is emerging. New social networks and digital platforms, new hiring, collaboration and marketing channels are replacing old ways of doing business. There are a lot of new structures that we can use to get by in this new world of work.

What if the biggest obstacle to success lies not out there, but in ourselves? Swiss psychiatrist Carl Gustav Jung, who pioneered modern personality theories, said we are all at risk of becoming too attached to the fictional image we create of ourselves. Jung calls it the "persona". We choose a profession and before we know it, we are trying to live up to the expectation of a role "which in reality one is not, but which oneself as well as others think one is," says Jung.[2]

"The danger is that [people] become identical with their personas – the professor with his text-book, the tenor with his voice. Then the damage is done; henceforth he lives exclusively against the background of his own biography."

Economists call such behaviour path dependency. We think we know who we are and what we're good at because we've studied a certain subject or worked in a certain field for years. Now circumstances are changing, but we're holding on to the professional identity we've created for ourselves because it's easier to continue on a set path than to walk on an entirely new one. Only, if we never look left or right, we don't notice the opportunities in unusual places. As with Adrián, the Spanish video producer who never thought he could be a university lecturer, the path can control us as blinders control a horse.

Let's free ourselves in two steps.

First, we need to accept that we are never just one thing. Join us over the next few pages to learn why the wisdom of a relatively unknown Hindu goddess holds a key for mastering a future we cannot avoid – one in which our working lives will inevitably be more fluid.

Next, we can make the most of our fragmented existence by boiling down a simple marketing strategy from the 1960s, known as the 4Ps, into the Flow Generation's secret sauce for success.

Unbox yourself! You are already broken

Anyone who thinks we should rely on the familiar structures of the past must also wonder why so many fixtures in our lives – politics, labour markets, media – look shaky and broken beyond repair.

What if nothing was ever whole to start with? Not the world around us and not even ourselves.

Philosophers like Heraclitus and Vico remind us that our cosmos, the order of all things, was born of chaos and keeps evolving, which means nothing ever stands still. Modern physicists, who study the strange behaviour of tiniest particles, have come to a startling conclusion: The world is not made up of solid things. It is a disordered succession of events that interact with each other. Like a kiss that happens but does not last, everything is always in motion, crumbling, transforming, becoming. "The world is made up of networks of kisses, not of stones", says Carlo Rovelli, a quantum physicist with the soul of a poet, in his illuminating little book *The Order of Time.*

It's a realisation that puzzles the most sober-minded scientists because it raises fundamental questions about human identity. If there are no entities, only processes and events, "What, then, am 'I'?" asks Rovelli, who draws on the laws of thermodynamics, the writings of Buddha, the myths of Hinduism and the wisdom of ancient Greece to find one logical answer: we, too, are nothing more than a collection of relations and events.

We may have formed a firm idea of who we are, based on the reflections we receive back from others and the memories and stories from our past. But our mind is playing tricks on us. We are as indefinite and in flow as the chaos around us.

This view has endured over thousands of years in Hindu mythology, which portrays the cosmos as an eternal river ruled by Shiva, the destroyer and restorer of all things. (Yes, rivers keep coming back throughout civilizations!) Hindus even have a special deity who represents our continuous state of flux. Images show her flowing gently down a river on the back of a crocodile, and her name sounds dark and mystical like a magic spell: Akhilandeshwari, the "Goddess Never Not Broken".

Never. Not. Broken.

What seems like a mind-bending paradox makes sense the longer you let it sit. Akhilandeshwari is always broken and never whole because nothing ever is. We ourselves are a set of moving pieces, a bundle of ever-evolving skills and talents, experiences and roles. It's important to remember this at a time when many people are worried about the unpredictability of the future of work. The old order is dissolving and our identity may seem at risk, but how can we break when we are already broken?

Akhilandeshwari reminds us that there is a lot of creative power in not being stuck in one form, nor neatly ordered, controlled or confined to one path. "Within that brokenness there is freedom," says Laura Amazzone, a mythologist. "The potential of what we are becoming is ultimately limitless."[3]

THE SAFETY NET OF MULTIPLE LIFE STRANDS

Thinking about it this way, the current turmoil in the world of work could be a blessing in disguise. Freed from the shackles of a nine-to-five office routine, we can finally come out of our box and use all our talents, skills and strengths whenever and wherever we like.

What if we have, not just one, but many vocations? What if, instead of identifying with one narrow job, we can identify with many? What if, in fact, we can live several different kinds of life, all at once? So let's reinvent ourselves and reassemble all our broken pieces until they fit the changing circumstances.

Pioneers of the Flow Generation have understood that the box-like career thinking of the past is a hindrance in the gig, sharing and data economy. So they decided they might as well break out of their path and do whatever they like. They are people who have already turned their back on life as "leashed office lemmings" to become job jugglers or digital nomads.

Among them are Alessandro Mazzi, freelance lawyer and kitesurf instructor, and Robert Crocker, who traded a corner office in San Francisco for a beach life in Bali. They embrace a career in flux because it opens them up to new experiences and allows them to uncover hidden talents. Job security, as they define it, does not mean having one job for life. It means constantly broadening your range and learning new skills to navigate uncertainty.

A large global survey by recruiting firm Manpower confirms that many young people have shifted to a new mindset that "sees individual jobs as stepping stones to self-improvement, rather than a final destination". Every fourth (27%) of the 19,000 millennials (between 20 and 34) surveyed across 25 countries said job security today means having job skills that match market needs. A jagged career replaces job security and acts as a safety net. "It's about the journey not the job," says the Manpower survey.

These millennials are frontrunners in the changing world. They are a step ahead of others who are still trying to figure out how to best live life in our increasingly fluid, digitalised and unpredictable times. There's much to learn from them, as we are all trying to find our flow in a new world order.

Can you solve this problem for me?

We need to unbox ourselves because the world around us is changing faster and faster. This doesn't mean we will all have to be job jugglers. The traditional full-time job will never fully disappear.

Many companies depend on permanent employees who show up every day to do their work and in return receive a regular pay check with all the usual corporate perks. In fact, companies including IBM and Yahoo recently reversed longstanding remote-work policies and called thousands of staff back to their office desks, in a much-debated move they said would enhance collaboration. Yet the demands on full-time employees are increasing.

We're facing a future where robots and AI will carry out most of our mundane work, while humans will do everything else: the complex problem-solving tasks that machines can't do because they require emotional intelligence, empathy and creative thinking.

What's behind those buzzwords? They mean that in the future, companies will recruit more people who can see beyond commonplace visions, who bring in ideas and experiences that challenge assumptions. People who can draw on a multi-faceted work and life experience to deliver the insights that help a company adapt and move forward.

Take Tim Fung, CEO and co-founder of digital work platform Airtasker. When he recruits talents for his team of 200 staff in Sydney, London and the Philippines he wants candidates to impress him with critical thinking more than a neatly formatted resumé. He challenges applicants to find a solution to a real-life problem related to his current business.

"Can you solve this for me?" he asks applicants and warns them straight away that he himself doesn't know the answer.

"This is what it means to think like an entrepreneur. No one is telling you how to solve a problem. You've got to figure it out yourself," says Fung, whose own career has been an experimental meandering that took him from investment banking to working in a fashion agency. He launched various startups before landing a hit with Airtasker, including a custom shirt design company and a motorsport event group.

A recent success story from Tim Fung's hiring practice: a 19-year-old who had no degree, but could solve technical problems more easily and cleverly than anyone Fung had ever met. He didn't hesitate to appoint the junior as technical team leader.

THE NEW SMARTS ABOUT MERIT

Employing people on merit, rather than academic background, work experience, race or gender, may not be mainstream yet, but it is a growing trend. Some of the largest companies worldwide, from tech giants Apple and Google to Starbucks and Ernst & Young, recently decided to drop the college degree as an entry requirement for new hires. Many others have done away with resumes and, like Airtasker, now evaluate candidates based on practical work sample tests.

Iris Bohnet, a behavioural economist at Harvard, is convinced that the old-fashioned hiring method based on written resumes and random interview questions ("Where do you see yourself in five years?") has no future.

Dozens of surveys show that traditional recruiting too often favours candidates that "look the part" or hold views similar to the interviewer's, rather than promoting the best person to actually do the job, she says.[4] Studies reveal that this bias can prompt male bankers to hire more male bankers and female teachers to hire more female teachers.[5]

Digital technology is changing this and Bohnet is a trailblazer for a future in which companies filter candidates based on talent not pedigree. She is advising several startups that provide new data analytics tools to assess which people would really thrive in a job, irrespective of their backgrounds.

One of these startups, London-based Applied, found that 60 per cent of the tens of thousands of job seekers who have so far sought work through its platform wouldn't have been hired with a typical CV.[6] These applicants were also more likely to come from diverse backgrounds. Applied is working with dozens of organisations worldwide, including publisher Penguin Random House, the UK Civil Service and hotel chain Hilton. In October 2018 they had reached a milestone of 50,000 candidates assessed for 2,000 jobs through their platform.

New-York-based Pymetrics, whose clients include consumer good producer Unilever, electric car maker Tesla and career portal LinkedIn, gets job seekers to play a set of neuroscience games to identify their core skills and personality traits. Algorithms then match candidates with suitable roles, regardless of past work experience.

Employers notice the difference. When one of the world's largest consultancies recently shifted to algorithmic hiring to manage a flood of 800,000 applications per year, the HR managers were surprised how flawed their human hiring processes had been.

"There has always been a huge focus on getting applicants from the top universities, but they were predominantly male," says Anna Breimer, an expert on modern hiring and workplace strategies who was involved in the consultancy's shift to robo-recruiting.

"The algorithm managed to overcome this gender bias by getting rid of the preference for top-school candidates. Suddenly 15 per cent more women jumped the application hurdle," she says.

Pymetrics founder Frida Polli, a neuroscientist herself, started the company out of frustration over her own career outlook while doing an MBA at Harvard. She said her academic resume conveyed nothing about what she could do in the business world, let alone that she could become a tech entrepreneur. "I was a 38-year-old single mom who didn't fit the 20-something, male entrepreneur mould."[7] There has to be a better solution, she thought.

The rise of startups that promote unbiased hiring follows the logic of digital platforms like Netflix, Spotify and Amazon, which use big data analytics to match a customer's traits with the best product. Why not use the same formula to match job seekers with their ideal job?

"The whole economy is now driven by data, but most people aren't using data to make career choices. They ask parents and friends for advice," says Tom Moore, CEO and co-founder of WithYouWithMe, a startup that specialises in recruiting talents for the booming cyber security industry in the US and Australia.

Relying on personal advice can be problematic at a time when traditional career paths are dissolving fast and new jobs are emerging that your parents may have never heard of: drone operator, mobile user interface designer, cyber resilience solutions architect.

There's a risk if you continue to look for jobs of the past. "The days of becoming a lawyer because your parents were lawyers are over," says Moore, whose startup applies a fiery mix of algorithmic skills assessment and combat mentality to get people from all walks of life – army veterans, underemployed bus drivers, former athletes, housewives and college graduates – high-paid jobs in cybersecurity.

Startups like WithYouWithMe, Applied and Pymetrics prove that anyone can succeed in any industry where jobs are being created, even without industry-specific work experience. These tech startups act as tailwind for the Flow Generation because they use data and algorithms to make it easier, not harder, for talented people to understand what they're good at and to find the right job.

In the age of artificial intelligence hiring is going high-tech, yet the future is less scary than the headlines about robo recruiters weeding out CVs suggest.

You can try to beat the machines by asking services companies such as Jobscan to pepper your resume with all the right keywords to increase your chance of making it through the computer barriers, also known as Applicant Tracking Systems (ATS). But if current trends continue, the written resume will eventually surrender to a hiring culture where an applicant's score in simulation games and data-based skills assessment tests become the door opener to a new job. It means the entire recruitment process becomes more permeable for career switchers.

This is the future of work: it will matter less and less whether you have followed a straight career path or not. What matters is that you have what it takes to solve a specific problem and be self-reliant in your decisions – whether you are a freelancer, contractor, full-time employee or task-based crowd agent.

The key question, again, has shifted from "what do you do?" to "what are you good at?". The future belongs to the independent worker and the jagged career.

The art of juggling jobs in four steps

One of the most striking similarities of the job jugglers and digital nomads we feature in this book is their ability to stop thinking like an employee. They think of themselves as their own best asset, a highly versatile product that can be positioned, priced, polished and promoted in various markets and situations. These people have not only redefined security to master a rapidly changing world. They have also redefined themselves. Knowingly or unknowingly, they have revived a classic marketing concept from the early days of mass consumption.

Dubbed "the 4Ps" by Philip Kotler, an American marketing professor in the 1960s, the framework has taken a little criticism in recent years. Some modern marketeers call it old-fashioned and unfit for our digital age, but that's not true. In our swiftly changing world, these precepts can serve as your secret success formula. The 4Ps are:

- **Product.** That's you, and who are you?
- **Price.** What are you worth and how do you receive compensation for it?
- **Promotion.** What's your brand and how do you convey it?
- **Place.** Where would you like to work and how do you make the change?

PRODUCT: BE LIKE JAZZ

The sounds of the saxophone swirl in the dark like fireflies, jolting from belly-deep lows to brain-piercing highs. And just when you think you found a melody, the tunes start dancing to a new rhythm from somewhere behind the screen with the flickering silent movie and the strobe light that bathes the DJ and the guitarist in streaks of red.

Slamjazz.

That's what the organisers named this weirdly fascinating spectacle that pitches six jazzmen and three slam poetrists against each other in a club in Prague, Czech Republic.

Job jugglers

"Totally experimental," says Jan Horky, a 38-year-old graphic designer, who hosted the event with a free-spirited collective of friends. It's an exercise in creative improvisation.

Jan smiles. Events like Slamjazz make him happy. Over the past few years, he has launched several art and music festivals, and there is no way his boss could persuade him to work full-time in his day job as an infographic and automation specialist. Jan enjoys his looser work week: three-quarters office safety and one-quarter freelance adventure.

"I want to be able to take off and do my own thing at any time. I want to be in control of my work," he says.

Since his wife had their second baby Jan is keeping a close eye on his bank account. Some of his many side projects pay off financially, others never do. Still, Jan takes them on because they offer him something invaluable: a creative outlet and a chance to learn new skills. In a way, Jan explores work like a jazz musician who only anticipate his moves – always ready to play but never knowing for sure if and when a tune will fit.

***

Researchers call Jan a "diversified freelancer". People like him earn money from various income sources, but keep one leg firmly in a traditional job. In the US, almost 60 per cent of the estimated 56.7 million freelancers in 2018 fell under this category, according to a survey by Upwork and the Freelancers Union.[8]

They are job jugglers like Afraz Adam, 39, who works part-time as a forensic doctor in Auckland, New Zealand, in order to have three other careers on top – as a pilot flying businessmen in charter planes across the rugged shores of New Zealand's main islands. As a casual TV actor. And as a certified entertainment doctor. When popstars from all over the world are in town, they book Afraz to treat their inflamed vocal cords or sprained ankles. He added this specialist qualification a few years ago, purely out of curiosity. "I'd be bored if I had to do only one job all the time," he says.

People like Afraz and Jan have diversified themselves like multi-use products that can be stocked in different stores and shelves and seasons and still always find a buyer. Their long list of talents and skills gained from hands-on experience serves as an insurance against the vagaries of work in the automation age.

Unlike many traditional employees, these job jugglers aren't afraid of the erratic tides of labour markets. They are constantly forging new paths and fostering new skills.

Robots may come, the Digital Revolution may continue, and jobs may change. But Afraz and Jan have created fallback positions for themselves. They feel in charge because they remain as fluid as the world around them.

Frank Barrett, an American management professor and jazz pianist, says the future belongs to those who know how to improvise. In his book *Yes to the Mess* he points out astonishing parallels between jazz music and job success. He describes how the world's best leaders and teams invent novel responses and take calculated risks without a scripted plan or a safety net that guarantees specific outcomes. Barrett says we have to master "the art of unlearning" in order to cope with the economic volatility and the rapidly evolving realities of our complex, hurried and globally connected world.

It's ironic how the gig economy of the 1920s is coming full circle. We are returning to the time when jazz bands would find their venues from Denver Ferguson's runners, as they roamed the streets of Indianapolis collecting lottery tickets. Now, we have digital platforms and data masses, but the basic premise is the same: we need the mindset of jazz musicians to master times of unpredictability.

This is the first lesson for future success at work:
Unbox yourself, stop identifying with one job and instead think of yourself as a product with various traits. Find out what these traits are and polish them. Then you can start selling them one by one or altogether, depending on the music that keeps changing around you.

PRICE: SELL YOUR SUPERPOWERS

If you are your own best product, how much are you worth? What do you write on your price tag in a rapidly changing world?

In the age of AI, any human work machines can do is devaluing fast. Meanwhile, the price of purely human work is rising. Research by consulting firm AlphaBeta shows that one hour of non-automatable work already pays 20 per cent more than one hour of automatable work.[9] While analysts calculated this figure based on Australian wage data, the overall trend is the same across the globe.

To claim a decent price in the automated future, you will need to stand out with skills that robots and other workers cannot easily mimic. It comes back to the question: what are you uniquely good at? The answer may not be as obvious as you think.

Career coaches report that many talented people are underselling their top strengths because they use them so effortlessly, almost reflexively, like breathing. They think hard-won skills are more valuable than these innate superpowers that come to them easily.[10] Others only haphazardly unearth their strengths – like Adrián, the Spanish film producer, who accepted the challenge to lecture at university and was surprised to learn he's good at teaching.

Or John, the cockroach killer, who arrived at Vera's doorstep in spring with a boxload of spray canisters, gel pumps and poisonous dust to shield her apartment against the legions of bugs that invade Sydney on long hot summer nights.

John, father of two preschool boys, is a diligent pest control technician, but his real strength is with people. Customers love his chatty personality. They send him raving reviews, and his boss rewards him with a 30-dollar gift voucher for each. "What's your secret?" colleagues keep asking. John doesn't know. He's just himself. After years of working in assembly lines and as a badly paid greenkeeper he never considered himself a people person. He never expected to excel as a customer service king in the cockroach-killing business.

John's attitude towards work fits the Flow Generation's success formula. He dares to experiment with different careers.

"It's not hard to find out what you're good at," said John when he had packed up and finished his cup of sugary tea. "But most people don't want to find out. They want to be told."

Not everyone is like John, Afraz, Jan or Adrián. Not everyone is prepared to venture into the unknown and explore talents left idle in their everyday work. For these people, a growing number of job-related data-analytics providers are offering professional skills assessments.

For instance, the American management consulting firm Gallup (better known for its polls) creates personal profile reports based on 34 strengths from strategic thinking to influencing to reveal what a person is naturally good at.

"This is your talent DNA," says Gallup in advertisements, and it recommends: "Stop trying to be more of who you're not, and start focusing on what naturally makes you powerful and unique."

Others, including the startups mentioned earlier in this chapter, combine skills assessments with a job-hunting service. They let algorithms figure out where candidates have the best employment and earnings prospects given their special strengths.

As long as you can prove that you're specialised and reliable, employers will pay you a premium – despite common fears that the gig economy will fuel a race to the bottom in wages.

Pay rankings show that top skills earn top dollars, even on digital platforms. Freelancers trained in spatial analysis, which can involve designing programs for self-driving cars, earned on average $110 per hour on Upwork in 2017.[11] Network analysts, who ensure all computers within a corporate network can communicate properly with each other, earned on average $200 an hour, according to Upwork.

At online work platform Airtasker, 60 per cent of employers hire not the lowest bidder, but the one who they think is most reputable, said CEO Tim Fung.

Labour market expert Stefano Scarpetta, Director for Employment, Labour and Social Affairs at the OECD in Geneva, says fears of widespread wage dumping in the platform economy appear overblown.

He also speaks from personal experience.

At a recent conference about artificial intelligence Scarpetta bumped into a fellow economist who had just tried his luck in the new world of hiring. Pressed for time and only hours away from his speaking gig, the man had posted an urgent call for help on one of the major online platforms. He needed someone to quickly finish a few PowerPoint slides – and received an avalanche of quotes in response. A designer from Pakistan charged $5 an hour. Someone from India asked for $12.50. And there was an American, who demanded $50.

"Economists would consider this a pretty well-diversified market," says Scarpetta. In the end, his colleague didn't choose the cheapest person, but the one whose reviews signalled the most consistent service.

Many employers hiring freelancers via online platforms want someone reliable and easy to communicate with. "Ultimately you want to establish a longer-term relationship," said Juan Arango, who runs a one-man services business for the construction industry on Australia's central coast. He has been contracting a Ukrainian web developer he found via Freelancer.com, always the same guy, for years now. "You don't want to be mucking around with people from overseas where you have to explain everything twice."

There is one caveat: the price you can charge remains tied to your reputation.

In the real economy, if your resume doesn't do the trick, you can now prove yourself to corporate recruiters in work challenges. However, if you sell your work via digital platforms, you need to build up trust by collecting positive client reviews.

Pioneers of the Flow Generation know that they need to pass a trust test before they can charge rates online that match the true value of their skills. Still in

South Africa, Alessandro Mazzi asked just $25 an hour for his legal services to get a foot in the door and attract his first client. Now, numerous clients and positive reviews later, he charges over three times as much.

It's the same promotional pricing model that brands use to attract buyers for a novel product. It's also what the new café in your neighbourhood does when it sells half-priced coffee for the first couple of weeks, hoping that customers stay loyal when the special sale is over.

Once established, the most successful job jugglers become iron-clad negotiators who know how much value they can create for a company and charge accordingly.

A clever coder, for example, who understands that his skills will significantly boost his client's sales, will demand not a meagre hourly rate, but a big-buck lump sum based on the total project value. It's the turning point from thinking like a dependent job juggler to thinking like a business.

This is the second lesson for future success at work:

To earn well, you need to get to know yourself. Find your unique strengths and the innate talents that come easily to you, but are difficult to automate. These are your most valuable traits. You may need to challenge yourself to become aware of all the superpowers you have within you. Prove that you have them and you can charge a premium, but be prepared to sell yourself at a bargain price until you've gained the trust and online credentials that the digital platform

PROMOTION: YOU GET WHAT YOU GIVE

Business management visionary Peter Drucker foresaw our era of self-management in the late 1990s, when he predicted that the 21st century would see a new breed of mobile knowledge workers "who must, effectively, be their own chief executives" to carve out their place and to know when to change course in uncertain times.[12]

Yet thinking and behaving like a chief executive is not enough in the digital platform economy. Workers also need to think and behave like salespeople. They have to promote themselves as a brand. It's challenging, as most people think of dodgy car dealers when they hear "salespeople" and feel uncomfortable when the product they're selling is themselves.[13]

What's more, building a brand can easily spiral out of your control these days. In the past, advertisers took a product, wrapped it in slogans and turned it into a brand. In the gig and sharing economy, the audience is in charge. What customers say, the reviews and ratings they leave online, can make or break a brand. No freelancer can succeed without a good reputation.

"It's like if people don't know you, you don't exist. If they don't talk good about you, you don't exist. If you haven't done any work at the top, you don't exist," says Adrián, the Spanish audiovisual content freelancer. He is constantly reaching out to old colleagues and contacts, hoping a job might manifest at some point.

A few flight hours away, in Thailand, Vietnam or Bali, the Flow Generation's most mobile members have taken a leap in self-promotion. Millions of Westerners have traded their corporate jobs for a roaming working life in tropical paradise. Almost five million Americans describe themselves as "digital nomads", according to a recent survey by MBO Partners.

They are like freelancers on steroids: skilled knowledge workers, storytellers and savvy salespeople in one. Digital nomads don't just sell a product or service

– they sell themselves and their life. Constantly on the lookout for business leads, they relentlessly feed social media a stream of glossy photos that create an enviable image of modern globetrotting professionals sustained by big dreams and digital technology: barefoot laptop creatives under beach umbrellas, framed by palm fronds and crystal blue sky.

The work-anywhere movement, while growing fast, is still in its experimental phase. Those who join it learn quickly that, in order to attract clients and build trust online, they need to turn themselves into a strong brand with a large followership of people who like and support their adventurous existence. They also learn to give freely, without thinking too much about what they might receive immediately in exchange.

Unconditional generosity is a mantra among digital nomads who have found that, in the end, the community universe will pay them back somehow. It's a core principle of modern attraction marketing in the gig and sharing economy: stop pushing people to buy. Instead, help to solve someone's problem because you care. Life is a give-and-take, and the giving part comes first.

The internet is full of freebies these days. You can download free e-books, access free tutorials, read free advice on platforms like Medium, or find free answers to your questions on Quora. Successful freelancers use all these channels to promote themselves and become trusted brands.

***

Dog whisperer, they call him. Some clients break down in tears as they watch him effortlessly gain control over animals they've known only as beasts. One sharp whistle, one firm gaze and the wildest hound obeys.

A trained chef and graphic designer, Carsten Wagner, 44, has always understood dogs like few others, but never thought of it as more than a hobby. He enjoyed giving free advice to fellow dog owners in the park. Some gave him 20 euros in return.

When the queries increased, he decided to promote himself in the same way. He launched a website and blog full of free information. He shot videos, added catchy teasers and posted them on Youtube. That was a catalyst. Suddenly, Carsten was getting calls from all over Europe.

Today, he charges proper fees as a dog trainer, but still loves his part-time job in a regional German school canteen as a safety net. He has gotten used to wearing earphones at work, always on standby to answer emergency calls from desperate clients with out-of-control pets. Then he pushes the kitchen cart with one hand down the school corridor, covering his ear with the other to blank out the clattering of cutlery and crockery.

"Just don't do what the average person does," he recently told the daughter of his long-term girlfriend. "When you're good, you will get booked."

This is the third lesson for future success at work:

In the gig and sharing economy you are the brand. What's your story? Make sure people take notice of you on social media, but don't mistake self-promotion with push marketing. The most successful people in the online universe give freely and share their knowledge abundantly to build a loyal followership.

PLACE: GO WALKABOUT

British researchers say we are witnessing a "spatial revolution" in the world of work. While newspaper headlines like "The office is dead" appear exaggerated, economists

Job jugglers

Alan Felstead and Golo Henseke from the ESRC Centre for Learning and Life Chances in London confirm that the remote working trend is no statistical artefact, but a real movement.[14]

More companies use technology to detach work from place. As a result, more people – not just tech experts, but also architects, marketing specialists, engineers, lawyers and teachers – can now work from anywhere. More than two-thirds of global employees work away from the office at least once a week and 53 per cent work remotely for at least half the week, according to a survey among 18,000 businesses in 96 countries by workspace provider IWG.[15]

The trend gives us a freedom that prior generations scarcely dreamt of. More people than ever have a chance to work wherever they feel most inspired, be it a vibrant startup city like Amsterdam or an Italian seaside village. Millions of knowledge workers have done the maths and moved to a remote tropical working hub. They now profit from a geographical arbitrage of earning Western dollars from Western clients in a low-cost developing country like Vietnam or the Philippines. Digital nomads inspire legions of others to reassess their own working lives.

Are you really happy where you are?

Websites like GoFuckingDoIt have begun to nudge dreamers to put their money where their mouth is. Just enter a long-held goal, set a deadline and vow to pay a dollar amount of your choice if you fail. While the platform never became a viable business, it raised $30,000 in pledges in less than a month after going live – a testament to the fact that we all have big dreams, and the only reason we may never live them is a simple lack of commitment.

Many pioneers of the Flow Generation simply have guts. They are not afraid of abandoning a script they once firmly believed in.

***

Ian Schoen calls it "jumping off the train" because that's how he felt, at 26, as an overworked product designer in San Diego, drafting in-store displays for sunglasses and watches. He realised that even if he kept going, even if he became the company's head honcho, he would at best end up in the top-floor office with views of the parking lot. And yet he was so invested: in his new car, his new clothes, the validation from colleagues, friends and family. Ian was like a passenger pulled along by a giant steam engine but no map.

How do you know what your strengths are if you can't see the start or finish line, only the little mechanism you've become in a big corporate machine?

Ian learned that once you reclaim the sovereignty over your life, you find the map again. "As an entrepreneur you have to see the big picture. You have to see the entire process from start to finish until you yourself become the big machine," he says.

Today, ten years later, Ian and business partner Dan Andrews support others in mastering the transition from a normal job to going solo. Their podcast The Tropical MBA began as a fun exercise to document the challenges and lessons learned when launching their own design and ecommerce company, a journey on which they often felt very alone.

Thousands of listeners have since tuned in, inspired by Dan and Ian's story, which they say "made for some decent, if lo-fi drama – a blue collar buddy flick. *Can these guys make it?*"

Job jugglers

We're no visionaries. We were two broke middle-class kids eyeing down many decades of 50-hour cubicle drudgery. We wanted to make great products, but we also wanted some control over our future.

Dan and Ian made it, so why can't others? Hundreds have joined their Dynamite Circle, a private community for location-independent entrepreneurs and world travellers in need of someone who shares their struggles and dreams.

"As long as cool people are getting together in the spirit of helping each other out, good things are going to happen," says Dan.

It is a myth that location-independent professionals are living an easier life than traditional employees. Their goal may be the *4-Hour Workweek*, glorified by author Tim Ferris, but a Wi-Fi link in the tropics isn't a voucher for slacking off.

Many digital nomads work harder on the road than they ever did in a regular office. Online 24/7 to juggle clients across time zones, many are battling to stay productive in an environment where every mosquito and every sunset can be a distraction.

Some are more fugitives than dreamers. They're running away from a corporate career confined by dress codes and power games. Yet they haven't clearly figured out what they want, other than to work less and do something they're passionate about.

"This place is full of broken toys," says the manager of a coworking space in Bali. He knows all the rags-to-riches stories that make the rounds on the island, tales from those who hit rock bottom – broke and depressed – until, miraculously, a person shows up who turns everything around.

Coworking spaces, now sprouting in every larger city in the world, become a lifeline against loneliness. Some have the flair of day care centres for grown-ups, offering an odd mix of coloured furniture, free juice, mastermind sessions and speed-networking lunches. But they are shaping up as hotspots for informal education, where independent workers learn new skills and exchange ideas.

The corporate office as the key arena for working and learning is losing its lustre. Diverse coworking arenas and digital platforms are filling the gap. No self-manager can afford to ignore the virtual space as a one-stop-shop for all professional needs. The internet is the new marketing canvas, vending machine, meeting place, recruitment fair, classroom, networking point and ideas exchange.

Digital marketing experts have a favourite saying: "The riches are in the niches." Adrián, the Spanish freelancer, learned it the hard way. He gave up offering his filmmaking skills on a major global gig work platform after employers there repeatedly tried to undercut his fee proposals. "They all wanted more work for less money," he said.

Things turned for the better when he discovered smaller freelancing platform Malt, which is only available in Spain and France and popular among creatives with design and tech focus. The narrower market was Adrián's advantage: clients were instantly more knowledgeable and appreciative, he said.

***

Sometimes the virtual space becomes a battleground. Signing up on a freelancing platform saved Shadi Al'lababidi Paterson's life as much as it almost destroyed it. That was a few years ago, when Shadi, now 24, roamed the streets of Bangkok with an aborted career as a professional poker player to his name and nowhere to go. For weeks he had been living off two-dollar street food that he bought in dingy curbside eateries. Still the bundle of cash in his pockets was getting thinner.

Shadi's fingers flicked through the notes. His savings wouldn't even get him home to England to finish university. Philosophy. What job do you do with a philosophy degree? A Seneca quote crossed his mind: *If one does not know to which port one is sailing, no wind is favourable.* Shadi paused. It might as well mean the opposite: if you have no clear destination but you have a sail, every wind is the right one.

Suddenly, he felt very optimistic. He could become anything the market would pay for. Coding was booming and Shadi learned the skills in long nights of self-study, surrounded by Bangkok's thick black night air. When he felt proficient enough, he joined Upwork and soon tripled his fees to $90 an hour, building a new career.

However, when one client complained after a string of miscommunicated emails, Shadi experienced the downside of the digitalised world of work. Upwork shut down his account and froze all his remaining funds, $2500. What's worse, the client threatened to leave a damaging review, a disaster in the gig and sharing economy where the online reputation is a freelancer's most precious asset.

At first Shadi felt helpless and mistreated, but then he decided to fight back – with social media as his weapon to mobilise a crowd. He published an entertainingly angry, yet diplomatically worded blog post on *Hackernoon* and *Medium*, two sites read by millions of like-minded, tech-savvy people. His story "Why you should never use Upwork, ever" went viral. Thousands shared it on Twitter and other online channels until his account was reactivated, his funds unfrozen.

"There's something about self-reliance that can't be undervalued. It is such an important trait, which you don't truly grasp until your back is against a wall," said Shadi, who today runs a successful growth marketing agency, The 8760, with partners in London and Kiev.

This is the fourth lesson for future success at work:

Technology has broken down the link between work and location. Today, the internet is the only place you cannot ignore anymore. Otherwise, the sky is the limit as the remote work movement gains speed. Are you inspired where you work right now? There has never been a better time to make a move to where you'd rather be.

The art of reinvention
will be the most critical skill of this century.
—*Yuval Noah Harari*

Chapter 6

Learning:

From set menu to snacks à la carte

The street sweeper's whistle cuts through the quiet that blankets Buenos Aires around dawn. Keep running, Alana thinks. Stay focused. Here, far away from home, Alana Leabeater, 22, is an attraction. The blonde exchange student from Australia. The lone runner training for triathlons when the rest of the Argentine capital is still fast asleep.

Strange how one can attract attention in one place but not another, she thinks. Next year, Alana will graduate with a double bachelor's degree in Sports Science and Arts in International Studies. However, the longer she thinks about it, the more she doubts that the formal education system has taught her anything to attract a decent job.

Life? Yes. Life has been a great teacher. The discipline that comes from being a competitive athlete, getting up at 4 o'clock to squeeze in a few hours of training before class. The just-deal-with-it moment she faced recently when, as a volunteer at the World Youth

Olympics in Buenos Aires, she was asked to be a Jill of All Trades: play tour guide for the Caribbean athletes, help dismantle the British team's wobbly bunk beds, and act as interpreter for the Spanish-speaking handymen who rocked with drills and saws and muscles, but had no command of the English language.

None of what she learned at school or university, all that memorising and regurgitating, prepared her for situations like this one, she says. "I just played the system. I just did exactly what the markers wanted", says Alana, who finished high school with grades better than 99 per cent of her peers in the country and is an exceptional student at university. Yet she fears she lacks the skills to cope with the modern workplace. In practical assessments she fares worse than her grades would suggest because she gets so nervous. And during a recent internship she struggled to accept critical feedback.

"I'm an employer's second choice: good on paper but doesn't deliver", she says.

What now? Alana is desperate to learn real-life skills: how to manage different people, change a car tyre, nail a job interview, buy a house, be entrepreneurial. On the other hand, she is worried that she will need to add more degrees – and student debt. When she recently applied for an unpaid internship, her competitors boasted a long list of titles. One even had a PhD.

LEARNING IS ON SPEED

Alana's worries are global. And they're not just on students' minds. People of all ages are wondering whether they've learned the skills to master the massive technological upheavals in our lives. Was my past education worth the money? Do I need another qualification to insulate me against job loss? Can I learn entrepreneurial thinking or do I have to have it in my blood? None of these questions are new, but they are more urgent today because knowledge decays like radioactive atoms, and technology is speeding up the process. Every new smartphone, every software update, every new machine in our economies forces us to delete parts of the old instruction manual that we once stored in our brains, falsely assuming that it might guide us through life.

Technology is changing our workplaces so dramatically that around half of the subject skills students learn in the first year of a four-year technical degree are outdated by the time they graduate, according to a popular estimate from 2007, which by now is probably also outdated.[1] Cyber security specialists say they need to update their skills every 12 months to stay ahead of the game.

The shelf life of knowledge will likely shorten further. Even less technical professions, such as teachers or marketing managers, might require very different skills in a few years from now as technology keeps changing the scene, according to research by the World Economic Forum.[2]

If we believe Israeli historian Yuval Noah Harari, the mid-21st century will almost certainly resemble our wildest idea of science fiction.

In just a few decades, we might all wear augmented-reality glasses at work that play training videos while we use our hands, connect us via live stream with colleagues, and let us see straight into someone's body – veins, bones, tumours and all.

Car assembly workers at Volkswagen and GE's aircraft maintenance crew are already using the technology.

Nobody knows if these dystopian visions similar to movies like *Ready Player One* or *Blade Runner* will become reality. We only know that we will work, communicate and move around differently. Cars will drive themselves. Software will translate and speak for us. Robots will dominate large parts our lives. We will use technologies not yet invented to perform jobs not yet created in an increasingly complex world, full of moving parts and contradictions.

It's not just the technological change that is keeping us on our toes. It's a powerful concert of forces that has been brewing over our economies like a storm: the globalisation, the outsourcing of jobs and offshoring of tasks, the new consumer desire for rapid on-demand service, as well as the unforgiving and ever-shorter cycle of fashions, trends and tastes. Pair these with the shifting work attitude of millennials and digital nomads who, in a rebellion against the linear career path, are happily jumping between roles, employers and countries, and you have a perfect recipe for unpredictability.

We simply cannot tell anymore how the knowledge we cram into our brains today will serve us in coming years. The jobs we once prepared for may not exist anymore, the skills we thought we needed may be irrelevant. We ourselves may have completely different ideas about how we want to work and live.

"The art of reinvention will be the most critical skill of this century," says Harari. "To keep up with the world of 2050, you will need to do more than merely invent new ideas and products, but above all, reinvent yourself again and again."

Learning is now on speed. It's as if the school bell never rings at day's end. And the confusion is high. What is the right education for a future where everything is in flux, where our bosses and recruiters are algorithms, where our careers are jagged and shifting, and where we will likely spend at least some time as freelancers and job jugglers?

A league of experts keeps making predictions. Just ask Google. Its search hits are full of numbered lists: the top ten dying jobs. The five best training courses to future-proof your career. Three skills robots will soon snatch from humans. Watch out, machines can now know your emotional state better than you yourself. Have you learned a coding language yet?

It's easy to feel that we have already lost the skills race against the machines.

MASTERS OF MISFIT

Our parents enjoyed some certainty. They taught us to look at life as a course we could divide into chunks. There was a school chunk, followed by a chunk of higher education or training, then a long chunk of work, which eventually led to a well-earned retirement chunk.

This simple model has broken down. One of Vera's girlfriends, a German TV producer, was flabbergasted when an older colleague recently took her aside and revealed: "You know I really can't be bothered to figure out all this new social media stuff. I only have 17 more years to retirement."

Only?

At the current pace of change, you could squeeze more careers into those years than our parents ever tried to fit into a lifetime.

Assuming you are complete because you've completed a chunk of education in your younger years has become risky in this world on speed. Even the value of a college degree, once the gold standard for professional success, is uncertain today, as Alana Leabeater and many others are finding out.

Economists frequently point out that higher education is still the safest bet to boost your job prospects and escape poverty. Statistics prove that people with a bachelor's, master's or doctorate earn more money and are more likely to be employed than people with lower qualifications. Over the past decade, the risk of being jobless with a college degree has even declined further.[3] However, the gap between what we learn at university and what we need to succeed professionally is wider than ever before.

The traditional college path now produces a lot of misfits. In the US, for example, more than 75 per cent of recent graduates in criminal justice are underemployed, which means they work in jobs that don't even require a college degree, official figures show.[4] In Australia, one in three young university graduates hasn't found work in their chosen field and one in five has lost hope of having a career they are passionate about, according to research from TwoPointZero, a youth career coaching firm.[5]

Italian university graduates under 35 have one of the lowest employment rates in the developed world. Just two-thirds of them are working. Only graduates in Saudi Arabia fare worse.[6]

What is going on? The common complaint is that something is terribly wrong with our traditional education system. It is obviously failing to prepare young people for the new reality of rapidly changing skills, jobs and career paths.

Anxious about not having enough credentials in their CVs, many keep loading up on them – another degree, a post-grad, maybe an MBA – until they are overeducated but underqualified for the reality of modern working life. Companies say they get candidates with a string of hard-earned letters after their names who can't solve real business problems.

An entire generation of young people seems to be learning the wrong things or at least things that companies don't appreciate. In a global survey by staffing firm Manpower, 45 per cent of employers complain that they cannot find people with the skills they need to fill open roles. Manpower says the worldwide talent shortage is the worst in over a decade.

There are signs, though, that companies are exaggerating. Peter Capelli, an American management professor and author of the book *Why Good People Don't Get Jobs*, says many employers today have unreasonable expectations and absurd applicant-screening software that kicks perfectly suitable applicants out of the running.

He describes the case of one company which had 25,000 applicants for a standard engineering position of whom the staffing people said not one was qualified. It sounds insane.

Still, employers worldwide are wringing their hands over the lack of talent. That's great news. It means there are jobs, but not enough matching skills. It means something can be fixed.

THROW OUT THE STALE OLD STUDY MENU

The demand for highly skilled workers remains intense, as employers are offshoring or automating more and more menial tasks (those that require little brains or craftsmanship).

However, when, where, how and especially which skills we need to learn has changed. Let's try to untangle the situation over the next few pages and cheer up because the world of education is probably the most exciting it's ever been.

We are freer in our education and career choices today than our parents ever were and our future is brighter than the scaremongering about dying jobs suggests, thanks to an explosion in new, fascinating online learning options and a nascent trend among employers to hire on merit, not degree.

Forget the idea that several years of studying will somehow prepare you for a lifetime of work. Forget the set menu that served education in one large chunk before entering the job market. Today, learning follows the piecemeal pattern of the on-demand and platform economy. As jobs break down into gigs, degrees crumble into a variety of snack-size course modules that are available online, downloadable on your smartphone, and consumable night and day.

Education is now a lifelong buffet, to which we return again and again for smaller portions whenever it suits our changing circumstances. It's a huge opportunity if we accept three major shifts in the way we approach education. We need to:

- Accept that learning has no more fixed space and routines. It happens everywhere and all the time.
- Forget the idea that one degree or skill will set us up for a whole working life. In turbulent times we need a mission not a major.
- Learn to rely on our inner compass and trust that everything is possible.

The old paths of education are crumbling, but new paths are already emerging. Rest assured that all the skills we need to pursue our dreams are right at our fingertips.

Where we learn: Loops, screens, talent gardens

YOUR PACE. YOUR TIME. YOUR LIFE.

A few years ago, design students at Stanford University's Hasso Plattner Institute of Design (fondly known as the d.school and famous for unusual thought experiments and provocative ideas on how to change the world) were asked to imagine what college learning might look like in 2025. They sat down with students in groups, talked about careers and life goals, drew straight lines onto flipcharts, then crossed them all out.

After months of research and brainstorming they presented sheets full of coloured scribble with lots of twists and turns and loops. The message: Life isn't a straight line so why should education assume it's predictable?

The Open Loop University the students invented fully embraces the new nature of work. Their visionary institution has no alumni, only lifelong members who come and go as they please while dipping in and out of work and study. This new breed of eternal student is on a never-ending journey of discovery, incessantly switching between paid gigs and internships, travel experiences and gap years, formal and online learning.

Why not loop out of uni after two years to volunteer with an aid organisation in Nepal, then join a tech startup for one year only to return to university for some more learning? Imagine how much richer group discussions would be if "loopers" of all ages came together to draw on a wealth of work and life experiences. MBA students already thrive in this type of learning environment.

That's exactly how the d.school team envisages the future for all students. A slogan advertising their loop

education model reads: "Your pace. Your time. Your life."
The vision they created is starting to become a reality
around the globe.

Education in the liquid life is already anything but
straightforward. Learning today happens everywhere,
all the time and often ad hoc. Universities and training
providers themselves are realising that lingering in
traditional courses for years fails to prepare students for
the fast-shifting, automated future. Many have begun to
modernise their curricula by adding more modular and
work-relevant study options.

To be sure, we still need deep expertise and profound
knowledge to succeed professionally. Doctors and
engineers, for example, need a formal certification and
must plough through years of theoretical study and
practical work to perform up to par in their fields.

Short-term courses also cannot compete with the
pay prospects of formal degrees. The average financial
returns of completing a traditional bachelor's, master's
or doctorate are still at least 40 per cent higher than
those of a short-cycle tertiary degree.[7] However, flexible,
bite-sized education continues to grow as more people
demand courses they can complete at any stage of their
careers.

Some universities are now serving education like
pizza, inviting customers to choose their favourite
topping. In Australia, for instance, the University of New
England has introduced a smorgasbord of flexible, short
classes for students who can assemble units from various
undergraduate and postgraduate degrees into their own
mini "bespoke course".

These personalised mix'n'match degrees help
students move with a fast-changing world, says Vice
Chancellor Annabelle Duncan. "We recognise that many

working adults are simply not able to commit to a full degree and we firmly believe they should have access to the parts of a university education they need most."[8]

THE CLASSROOM IN FRONT OF YOU

The trend towards à-la-carte learning is threatening traditional universities as fortresses of education. An explosion of new, short-term study options is creating unprecedented competition in the education market. Some Australian university leaders interviewed by consultancy EY estimate that around 40 per cent of existing formal degrees could soon be obsolete.[9]

Education providers large and small are rushing to meet the growing demand for flexible, self-paced learning. Many use the same digital platform technology that matches Uber drivers with passengers and Airbnb hosts with guests.

Some of the world's most prestigious institutions, including America's top universities whose ultra-selective admission rules have long been shrouded in mystery, now give away their famed education for free on digital platforms such as edX or Coursera. Anyone anywhere can enrol in these "massive open online courses", or MOOCs, without having to pay big bucks or flying around the world. Others, such as the University of Ottawa, are offering entire "virtual" degrees online.

The internet is your classroom. There's YouTube, the new go-to channel for the hobbyist, featuring all sorts of free fix-this-fix-that videos from how to prune a lemon tree to how to unclog a toilet. Online learning platforms Udemy or Khan Academy make highbrow topics palatable for the layman ("The A-Z in Machine Learning"; Best of World History in six episodes). MasterClass lures with celebrities: cooking with

Michelin chef Gordon Ramsay or filmmaking with Hollywood director Martin Scorsese. Even tech giant Google has launched its own online training ground with certified courses. It aptly calls it Digital Garage – like a tool shed where workers can hope to find the right equipment in form of short video tutorials to fix knowledge gaps in digital marketing, coding or general career development.

The abundance of choice is great news as we get used to the liquid life, in which nothing is set and everything is possible. The expanding universe of modular learning is a huge opportunity for the growing number of freelancers, job jugglers and independent workers. Never before have we had so much easy and affordable access to high-quality education.

"For the first time in history, everyone has the opportunity to learn from the best in the field," says Shani Raja, a former *Wall Street Journal* editor, who runs some of the most popular writing courses (200,000 subscribers and counting) on Udemy and LinkedIn Learning. Everything we ever wanted to know is now available at a mouse click, and a lot of it is free.

"There is no more excuse for not learning," says Lachlan, the personal trainer who last year reinvented himself once again to start an online marketing agency Lachlan Media.

He draws on his own entrepreneurial experience and lots of self-study to help businesses quickly grow their internet presence and sales. Sometimes he spends half of a 10-hour working day just learning, reading, attending virtual classes. Many of the Flow Generation's pioneers operate just like him.

***

Rob Crocker takes out the earphones to watch the sun sink into the haze over the rice fields. Outside, the labourers are still mixing cement, putting final touches on Canggu's newest coworking space Outpost. Rob barely noticed them work all week. He was online, learning whatever came his way. He finished a creative leadership course on the education platform Skillshare, tuned into an art director's podcast on "Dangerous Ideas", completed brain games on Lumosity and bought tickets to an upcoming visual design conference in Miami.

"It pays to be an expert, and in order to become an expert you have to invest a significant amount of time into practice," says Rob, who has developed a strict system for structuring his love for learning. Before enrolling in a class, he asks himself: does it really help my career objective? If it doesn't, Rob lets it go.

On a recent ride into the mountains he finished an audio book called *The Laws of Simplicity*.

"Did you know you can get through loads of books by listening to them at double the speed?" asks Rob. "It might take some time getting used to, but once you're there everything else feels VERY slow."

***

Clearly not everyone who is offering ebooks, tutorials and courses online is worth their money.

The internet has made it easy for amateurs to brand themselves as experts, Instagram marketing gurus, motivational speakers or coaches, and some educational offerings have the smell of Ponzi schemes, warns Jochen Mai, founder of Karrierebibel.de, one of Germany's largest career service websites with 3 million monthly readers.

"Some people sell you a dream only to finance with it their same own dream," says Mai.

Yet education has never been as transparent as today. The new etiquette of writing reviews for everything and everyone in the digital platform economy, including course providers and professors, is making it easier to discern between quality education and scams.

LEARNING AT WORK

The boundaries are increasingly blurred between learning in a classroom and at work, between learning online and in real life. Labour market experts confirm what Alana Leabeater and others are realising the hard way. University can teach you "bonus skills" such as reasoning and research as well as team work and time management. But with some skills, particularly IT and problem solving, the best classrooms are the job and real life.[10]

Front-loading years of formal education at the start of adulthood appears increasingly out of step with reality. In fact, you might be better off learning a trade or getting any other practical work experience first. Official data shows that in countries including Australia, Czech Republic, Germany and the United Kingdom employment prospects for those who have completed a vocational training are on par with university graduates.[11] This is partly a result of cleverly designed work-and-study programs, such as Germany's *Duales Bildungssystem*, that simultaneously teach apprentices theory and hands-on skills.

These programs only exist in a few countries, but for the Flow Generation's pioneers this is no obstacle. They don't wait for institutions to change. They just harness the freedom of today's globalised labour markets to create their own work-and-study experience.

***

For Christmas they decorated the olive tree in the courtyard with paper lanterns and orange light bulbs until its naked branches looked like they were bearing fruit. Mattia Mammoliti could see the colours glow far down the gravel road that leads into the Apulian village where locals eat stuffed charcoaled peppers for dinner.

One day, he thought, he would buy all the olive trees on his parents' farm and beyond. He would turn them into a thriving restaurant business, selling oil and his own food: handmade pasta, fresh vegetables, sizzling meat.

It's been years since Mattia left his career as a fashion photographer to become a chef. He had finished his three-year studies at the Istituto Europeo di Design in Turin as one of the ten best of 100 students.

Strangely, though, his accomplishment felt threatened even on the day he graduated. Camera technology had advanced, the internet had expanded, social media had become a photo dump.

"I realised that what they taught me was already old," said Mattia.

The number of digital images taken worldwide has more than tripled to 1.2 trillion per year since 2010, statistics show.[12] The data boom is putting pressure on photographers. Many are left with only seconds to edit each shot.

Mattia adapted. For six years he worked freelance for big brands like Gucci and Kappa, but the stress to feed social media on speed dimmed his enthusiasm. Passionate about cooking since his dad taught him the basics as a child, he decided to change. This time he approached education from the tail. He asked himself, "Where can I get real-world skills fast to open an olive farm and restaurant?" He made a list. Then he went hunting for work experiences that would fill his knowledge gaps.

At 32, Mattia travelled from Italy to Sweden, inspired by the creativity of Nordic chefs who know how to cook rich meals with just the few ingredients that grow in their vast cold land.

He learned to make bread in Stockholm's best bakery because "without understanding pastry, you don't understand pasta". Later he joined a prestigious rotisserie restaurant to decode the secret mix of timing and temperature that grills meat to perfection.

Mattia believes in short, intensive, hands-on learning experiences. His work stints rarely last longer than half a year, but they take him out of his comfort zone and teach him something new. The downside is that he has to start over and over again at a low entry pay. It's a trade-off, but Mattia believes his financial sacrifice will pay off once he opens his own business.

Wouldn't he want to attend a cooking school?

"Why?" asks Mattia. "You don't need to be in a class to learn. Just find the best person you can learn from, someone who is passionate about the work you want to do, and listen."

COWORKING: THE PLAYGROUND OF LEARNING

Coworking spaces have become sites where digital nomads, freelancers and entrepreneurial thinkers exchange ideas, inspiration and skills. They bond over their shared belief that they can achieve anything they want and support each other's ventures with tribe-like commitment. Knowledge flows freely in coworking spaces. The question "What are you good at?" is a door opener. Noticeboards are crammed with notes proposing skill trades: "Seek accounting help, offer yoga class."

Shared office spaces also offer much-needed orientation at a time where we are inundated with educational content. Freelancers are cut off from standard corporate training sessions, and could spend weeks watching TED talks, reading ebooks and completing online tutorials without knowing whether any of this knowledge will ever serve them.

Aware of the dilemma, major coworking chains seek to become trusted guides and offer free workplace training as part of the membership.

A desk at WeWork in Amsterdam or Dojo Bali automatically gives you access to courses on anything from speaking Turkish to managing savings or "living with ease, flow and fulfilment".

Talent Garden, a global coworking chain, goes a step further by facilitating seamless learning at the heart of the digital economy. Its shared work spaces, often refurbished industry lofts in two dozen cities from Bucharest to Dublin, are open day and night and marketed as "campuses" where freelancers and students can collaborate with businesses of all sizes.

Partnering with big tech companies including Google, Cisco Systems and Vodafone, places like Talent Garden may become serious rivals to universities. Its range of master's degrees, lectures and workshops are designed to teach students the core skills that employers currently demand. Several corporations send entire employee teams here for training in growth hacking or data analysis.

Even more visionary is the educational concept of H-Farm, a startup incubator and campus nestled in the cow pastures near Venice. H-Farm hosts a primary school (where children learn three languages and coding), a breeding ground for startup businesses, as well as a university-level academy offering advanced technology classes in anything from robotics to data science.

People learn in small huts made of cement and glass, with the Alps as backdrop, but the ideas born here are big. The entire space seems like a giant experiment in education that knows no boundaries, only fluid curiosity across generations and occupations. Here, digital entrepreneurs, consultants, teachers and students come together to work and learn side by side.

Smartphones look old-fashioned in this place where even six-year-olds are wearing virtual reality headsets in class. A few fields away from the children's school lies the BlackRock Institute of Magic Technology, where grown-ups in their twenties learn how to create computer graphics, concept art and virtual reality software that make it into Hollywood movies or industrial design.

Some of these IT engineers develop virtual versions of a shoemaker's workshop (where Adidas customers can make their own sneakers). Or they build software that teaches electricians how to repair a faulty power grid during a thunderstorm. No one needs to get wet, of course. To complete a virtual reality training at H-Farm, you just need goggles, gloves and high-speed internet.

What we learn: Mindset and mission, not major

CULTIVATE BEING HUMAN IN A ROBOTIC WORLD

When surgeon Tim Peltz enters the operating theatre, steps muffled by the plastic cover on his shoes, he mentally prepares for the worst-case scenario: a power outage that would disturb all the high-tech utensils of modern medicine. Cables are hanging from the ceiling and a small trolley carries an assortment of electric scalpels. There are ultrasonic coagulation devices, computerised ventilation machines and intelligent software that tells Tim precisely how to cut tissue.

With all the machines in the surgery, Tim realises how much he matters as a person. No automation technology can replace one of his biggest skills: to calm a patient's nerves before the operation.

The thought of a robotic doctor scares the hell out of people, he says.

***

Economists and futurists at every large consultancy, recruitment firm, tech company and international organisation agree that our uniquely human traits, those that even the most sophisticated technology cannot replicate in a meaningful way, will become more important in the automation age. They include our creativity, our ability to solve complex problems, our ability to distinguish fake news from real information, our empathy and our compassion.

Across all industries social skills will be in higher demand than narrow technical skills, such as programming or equipment operation and control, according to research by the World Economic Forum.[13] Andrew McAfee, a research scientist at the Massachusetts Institute of Technology and co-author of the book *Race Against the Machines*, says jobs and tasks that will remain least affected by technology are the ones that tap into our "social drives".

In a world that feels loose and unpredictable and that is governed by algorithmic rationality, our success as humans will depend on how well we can manage the murky world of feeling: how good we are at encouraging, motivating, comforting and alleviating fears. How well we respond to emotional needs – those of others and our own.

In the 1968 sci-fi novel *Do Androids Dream of Electric Sheep?*, which inspired Ridley Scott's movie *Blade Runner*, writer Philip K. Dick imagined a post-nuclear-catastrophe world where robots are programmed with feelings. In another science-fiction book, *Ready Player One*, the protagonist finds himself so lost and lonely after breaking up with his girlfriend that he seeks comfort in his virtual assistant, only to feel even more lonely when the computer runs out of pre-programmed replies.

While computers are getting good at tasks like determining people's emotional states by observing their facial expressions and vocal patterns, they are a long way from understanding complex emotions like embarrassment, envy, pride and fear, says McAfee.

Androids can't give you heartfelt hugs. Humans can. The same goes for many other uniquely human skills we are told are critical for the future: generating original ideas, establishing and cultivating client relationships, managing teams. Computers can't deal with the unpredictability of human reactions. They fail to complete tasks for which no instruction manual exists.

***

The smell of pizza mixes with the incense from the nearby temple and it brings back memories of a time when Rob's life derailed. He had been travelling down Australia's east coast for months, desperate to establish himself as a freelance visual consultant, without winning a single major client. It was 4 am in the dark empty lobby of a startup hub in Sydney, when Rob, who never eats fast food, devoured the cold leftovers of someone else's pizza.

He felt like vomiting. "What am I doing?" he thought. "What's wrong with me?"

That was before he realised his nausea was actually fear. Fear of the future. It was before, still shaky, he made a new list of life goals and reassessed his funds and skills. It was before he admitted to himself that Australia wasn't for him, that he was on the wrong track and that he'd be better off in Bali.

That night Rob learned the biggest lesson about what it means to be a human in a robotic world. He came to terms with the frailty of his own self.

A MISSION, NOT A MAJOR

We need to let go of the rigid idea that there's a direct path to a particular dream job. We need to let go of the idea that there even is one dream job. In the liquid life our final destination has become a moving target. Like Rob, who changed course various times, we must accept that we are now on a lifelong journey of discovery spanning multiple jobs, careers and status changes on LinkedIn.

We're the Flow Generation. We are not fixed. Nothing is forever. And no one single degree can set us up for life. We must expect detours and distractions, roadblocks and restarts, even if we once had our eyes firmly set on one specific career. Circumstances will change and we ourselves will change in ways we cannot foresee.

We don't know where we might end up in three, five or ten years. It changes the outlook on what we should learn to be successful. Above all, we need to learn how to manage the new, faster, less predictable flow of our careers. The British philosopher Alan Watts, who was a cult figure in the 1950s and 60s among America's "beat generation" for popularising Zen and Buddhist teachings to a Western audience, once summarised it neatly. The essential principal of business, of occupation in the world, is this, he said: "Figure out some way in which you get paid for playing."

Of the many disillusioned Australian youths who call career coaching service TwoPointZero in Melbourne, most are surprised to find untapped powers within themselves. "We teach people how to fish. We don't feed them fish," says CEO Steve Shepherd.

Research by strategy consulting firm AlphaBeta and commissioned by the Foundation for Young Australians signals that students today might be better off focusing not on one job but on a whole group, or "cluster", of occupations that require very similar skills.[14]

Would you believe that a childcare worker, a surgeon and a beauty therapist have quite a bit in common? While each needs specific subject knowledge, they essentially all seek to improve the health or wellbeing of others and use a surprisingly large number of identical skills to do their job, from communication and case management to attention to detail, the study shows.

When we pick up basic "portable" skills, those that are useful for several jobs at a time, we boost our long-term success in this complex world. Then we may shift easily between an average of 13 different jobs within one occupational cluster, according to the research.

You could be an environmental research scientist, but the portfolio of core skills you've gained in that job would also make you fit to work as a medical administrator, fire officer, life science technician or zoologist. You will need some additional, job-specific training before you'd be competent in the new role, but rest assured: you already have the basics covered.

In the future, being a curious, knowledgeable individual with many different interests will count more than being a narrow-minded subject specialist. We're witnessing a shift to what education experts call purpose learning.

"The idea is to declare a mission, not a major," says Jess Munro, a lecturer at Stanford University and a design lead on the Stanford2025 project that explored the future of college. "You have to ask yourself what purpose you bring to the world."

Westerners should look to Africa for inspiration about what the future of education could look like. The African Leadership University, with campuses in Mauritius and Rwanda, is positioning itself as a global pioneer in purpose learning, announcing that students need a more "holistic experience" to succeed in an ever-changing world, in which "narrow academic theory quickly loses relevance".

There are no more lectures at the ALU, only self-paced, self-driven learning that breaks down barriers between universities and the real world. Students come together like novice entrepreneurs to solve real problems for real organisations.

The tasks they are confronted with challenge them to dive into various disciplines from anthropology to engineering and economics as they see fit. They are asked to discover for themselves what they must know to solve a problem, find the people with that knowledge, and learn from them. Essentially, they practice what photographer-turned-chef Mattia has recognised as the most effective way to learn new and relevant skills.

Teachers? Gone. At this university there are only "faculty facilitators" who guide students to become confident, self-reliant leaders by exposing them to the real life. Students spend eight months on campus and four months in a workplace of their choice, ensuring they have a whole year of work experience by the time they leave uni. Employers help to develop the curriculum.

It's a unique way of learning and a better fit for the liquid life, in which many of us are left swimming on our own – as independent workers without a pre-set path.

This African university is among the pioneers in teaching students how to chart a path themselves. It encourages them to declare a "mission for life", which then becomes their personal beacon for shaping a career in a changing world.

Such a purpose could be to design more liveable cities. To make our economies fairer. Fight poverty. Or simply to make more people smile and feel good about themselves. Once you have found your life's purpose, you can align your learning with it, says ALU.

Graduates from this university will not tell you they've studied engineering, because when they finish studying they will have gained more than a degree. They've become the versatile problem solvers that today's world requires.

They might surprise you by saying they've studied how to feed the world's hungry. It might sound provocative and visionary, but it's real.

Can you imagine?" asks d.school's Jess Munro, who is experimenting with similar learning strategies to prepare her students for the "incessant murkiness" of our lives. "In the future you might say 'I went to the School of Hunger'."

The power of resilience

MAKE THE CAPTAIN'S CALLS

What is your mission? The new purpose-driven approach in pioneer institutions like d.school or ALU is revolutionary because it puts the individual in charge. These institutions step aside to turn students into leaders who are skilled at solving complex problems with limited resources – and who dream big, in whichever field they go into.

There is a common belief that just a lucky few are born with the right entrepreneurial spirit, emotional resilience and zeal to make the most of the mounting uncertainty, while the vast majority of us seem cursed with some sort of "employee gene" that hinders us from standing strong in our own ideas and inspirations against the uncertainties of our accelerated world.

Pioneers of the Flow Generation defy this assumption. They prove that all of us already carry within us the means to forge our own path and persevere in a world where nothing is fixed: not our career, not our education and not ourselves.

They teach us that there are two ways of dealing with the increasing performance pressure and chaos around us. We can remain reactive and try to keep up with the forces that are tossing us about, but it will be emotionally exhausting and difficult to sustain in the long run. Or we can put on the captain's hat and chart our own course through increasingly rough and unpredictable waters.

It's a challenging task because it requires us, even if we work in a secure full-time corporate job, to listen more carefully to our own inner compass at a time when many of us feel trapped in a rat race with the mounting demands of the modern workplace. Employees are overwhelmed and stressed like never before. Burnout has become "just part of the job" for many, says research firm Gallup.[15] Many complain about unmanageable workloads, unreasonable time pressure and lack of support from their managers.

Those who are already most at ease with the new fluidity of life – Czech job juggler Jan or German dog trainer Carsten – look inwards before they look outwards for direction. They start with a question made popular by one of the world's most intense business leaders, Apple co-founder Steve Jobs: "What makes your heart sing?"

The pioneers of the Flow Generation make captain's calls. They're not passively bobbing around, waiting for bosses or circumstances to change, or for friends and family to give them permission. Rather, they ask themselves whether it might be time to reroute their lives and then they "just go fucking do it", trusting that everything they need to learn is available online at any phase of life.

Many of them then discover something surprising: pursuing a path you really deeply believe in, something that motivates you so much that it almost lifts you out of bed in the mornings, can give you superpowers. It can suddenly, magically, equip you with all the skills future-of-work experts agree we must have to successfully master the liquid life – skills such as being entrepreneurial, flexible, disciplined and resilient, being able to solve complex problems, being eager to learn, willing to take risks, and overcome failure.

There's never been a better time to carve out your dream career because entry hurdles into higher education are disappearing just as workplaces are opening up to hiring a wider range of talent based on merit, not degree. It's never been easier to reach for the stars in this new, digitalised world of self-paced education and work.

THE MAGIC OF GRIT

There is a common mantra, perpetuated by hundreds of self-help books, that we only need to "find our passion" or "discover our purpose" and we'll glide on to success. However, it's foolish to think that there's a magic button that will activate our unique personal talents and passions and finally give us boundless motivation to sail through any difficulties.

"Passion is bullshit," says American cartoonist Scott Adams, whose comic strips about the frustrated office worker Dilbert and his pointy-haired boss capture the madness of corporate life like no other.

In his book *How to Fail at Almost Everything and Still Win Big*, the cartoonist recalls more than a dozen business ventures he was involved in. He once opened a restaurant, designed computer games, published a beginner's guide to meditation. At the start his passion was always sky-high, he says. But when a venture didn't work out, and most of them didn't, his initial excitement turned into frustration and annoyance.

It's true that having a purpose – an intention to contribute to something bigger than yourself – and a burning interest can spur us to unexpected heights. However, we need not just a purpose and passion. We also need a strong dose of perseverance to master the liquid life. We need what US psychologist Amanda Duckworth famously called "grit", an endless reserve of willpower and focus to overcome obstacles and reach a goal even in the face of significant adversity. Duckworth found that grit is the real secret to life success, more so than talent or intelligence.

Grit keeps a captain on course as he makes his journey through unmapped territory and choppy seas. We all need grit if we want to stop our personal dreams from being just a fantasy.

***

Sometimes life puts you to the test: How badly do you want something? Do you keep going when you fail once? Twice? Three times?

Lisa Aizenberg failed the annual admission test to become an Australian firefighter four times in a row. Yet she kept coming back each year, as if to prove that the authorities had made a mistake, that no one on earth had the right to mess with a personal dream that Lisa saw written in the stars.

Becoming a firefighter had been her childhood dream. Astronaut or firefighter. But as so often with childhood dreams, Lisa forgot about it. Instead, she started working in the hospital her dad was managing, helping out in the canteen, assisting the physios. It was a job, all right. It paid the bills and the drinks on weekend nights out with friends. Until one day the dream returned. Lisa was 25 and bored at her desk in a ward full of sick people, a windowless room with walls painted in calming colours, when she remembered: firefighter.

Firefighters need to be sharp as machines. They make life-or-death decisions in a split second. They need to be strong, physically and mentally. So Lisa began to prepare for the highly competitive entry test. She is only 1,62 metres tall, dwarfed by the big blokes in uniforms who drag water-heavy hoses into burning houses and injured humans out. Lisa started lifting weights. She also bought *Maths for Dummies* because she had forgotten how to do simple calculations in her head.

Year after year she missed the mark. Yet "every time I failed, I was getting closer to passing," says Lisa, who vowed to try harder each year. In the fifth year, she says only some 70 of around 10,000 applicants made it. Lisa, finally, was one of them.

Her mum told her she was running into something others run away from. "It's so true," says Lisa, smiling. "I'm running into flames."

***

Gritty people like Lisa don't give up at the first setback. They put in a sustained effort over a long time because they are so strongly motivated by what they do. They hold on to their vision against all odds.

The world's best hero stories are built on grit. It kept the Airbnb founders glued to the belief that people would pay to sleep on an air mattress in a stranger's home, despite investor scepticism.

The same grit helped The Tropical MBA founders Ian and Dan endure months of loneliness and doubt at first. Ian said neither of them knew how to record a podcast or run a business, but they were convinced they could make it happen. "It didn't matter if I was good at it because I knew I was going to work harder than everybody else," said Ian.

Interestingly, we all have grit. All of us. Like optimism, grit is an innate psychological trait that we can develop. We may have forgotten how gritty and self-reliant we can be, as we have gotten used to a world with fixed career paths, strong institutions and functioning safety nets. Remember how, as children, we could immerse ourselves for hours in an activity without getting tired, doing somersaults or practicing skateboard jumps until dark? The liquid life gives us the freedom to start playing again. Once we play, once we do what we really enjoy doing, the grit automatically kicks in.

The powerful mix of passion, purpose and perseverance also fosters something else: strong and unlikely human connections that help us stay on course. As soon as we do what makes our heart sing, we create a powerful social pull that is critical for survival in a world where traditional education chunks are dissolving, says a team of Deloitte management consultants in their acclaimed book *The Power of Pull*.

Success no longer comes from possessing stocks of knowledge that we once carefully built up and stored away. Today, knowledge flows all about in streams and we must learn to tap into them. We must draw out like-minded people and resources from around the globe to create our own flow of knowledge for each endeavour, the authors say.

THE IMPOSSIBLE IS NOT IMPOSSIBLE

In the early days, no physician ever thought people could dive beyond 100 metres with just one breath in their lungs. The pressure grows so intense on their ribcage that eventually, science said, it would crush them.

French freediving champion Guillaume Néry has proved science wrong many times. He has managed to reach deeper and deeper depths, sinking to 139 metres, his body so compressed it falls into the cold dark blue like a stone. And when he touches the bottom, all alone surrounded by suffocating water masses, a tiny drop in a vast ocean, something strange happens: he feels extraordinarily well, without any need to breathe.

Extreme athletes like Néry stretch the limits of the body with the power of their minds. They say freediving is, above all, an inner journey. All those limiting beliefs

humans like to impose on themselves, the earthly re-
flexes to fight and resist pressure, don't work underwater. The only way to survive is to give in to the elements and control nothing but yourself.

"I let the water crush me," Néry told an audience in
Toulouse during a galvanizing TED talk. "I accept the
pressure and I go with it."

In the Mediterranean off the French Côte d'Azur,
job juggler Alessandro Mazzi could relate to the champion's words as he tried freediving himself. The air
smelled like autumn, but the water was still warm, and
Alessandro learned to stop breathing, for minutes. He let
the pressure crush him, shut off his mind – and felt inex-
plicably alive.

Old friends, with a mix of jealousy and admiration,
say he's living the dream. They see the photos he posts
of himself kitesurfing and freediving and speaking at
international conferences. What they don't see is that he,
too, had to stay extremely focused to get as far as he did.
It involved a lot of suffering, he says, including a month
of cleaning toilets in a Dutch hostel. "You have to believe
in your power and relax," says Alessandro. "It's a mental
process."

***

For the Flow Generation's frontrunners the impossible is
not impossible. They simply trust that they have
unlimited potential to reinvent themselves and vaporise
the limits of what they or others once thought would be
a suitable career, job or profession for them. It's critical
that we stay open-minded about different work and
learning opportunities in these rapidly changing times.
We must be broader and more adaptable than previous
generations. We must explore new avenues at all times

and relentlessly soak up new skills and knowledge, often in areas outside our core expertise and in subjects for which we may think we have no talent.

Then it depends on our attitude. Do we shy away from reinventing ourselves because we think, "This is not my thing"?

Or do we remember Hindu goddess Akhilandeshwari's wisdom that we are always a sum of broken pieces, all of which have equal potential to become a strength?

A team of researchers around Stanford psychologist Carol Dweck says our common definition of passion is problematic. If we think we are born with a fixed set of talents and passions, we may focus only on a narrow range of pursuits that come easily to us – and chuck the rest into the "too hard" basket, falsely assuming that we're just not carved out for them. The truth, the researchers say, is that we can develop many passions if like a freediver we overcome the boundaries we have created in our heads. Anything that tickles our fancy has the potential to become an intense interest that blazes a path ahead of it.

Some universities actively foster this "growth mindset". The *Studium Fundamentale* at German university Witten-Herdecke, for example, nudges students to use 10 per cent of their mandatory study time to explore subjects and classes beyond their ordinary degree.

The Irish University College Dublin has created a similar program called Horizons. Participants like 21-year old Orla Keaveney feel optimistic about the future because they can already spread their courses widely as part of their degree. Orla is studying electrical engineering, but has also taken classes in film style & aesthetics, applied psychology and creative writing. She works as a casual reporter for a local newspaper, but who knows what the field will look like by the time she finishes her studies? A journalism or production course never appealed to her with all this rapid technological change, she says.

"Electronics seemed like a way to be in the loop with evolving technology rather than trying to keep up," says Orla, who likes to stay versatile. "My dream job would be to sort of straddle between tech and media, maybe doing freelance work in both fields for a bit before settling into whichever suited best."

The future belongs to the growth mindset. It's just a matter of switching it on.

Ask Samaschool, a San Francisco-based training program that teaches unemployed and underemployed Americans the basics of freelancing. It proves that anyone – even marginalised people with a history of low-income jobs – can learn to shift into "no limits" mode and acquire key entrepreneurial skills.

Tech companies Adobe and Google support the non-profit, which collaborates with online education provider Udemy and gig work platform Fiverr.

Its mission: empower people to create their own work instead of getting frustrated by the elusive chase for a full-time standard job in the growing gig economy. Its trainees: a few thousand people per year, some of whom are used to earning just enough money to make a living.

Samaschool helps them to think in possibilities. They learn the skills they need to succeed as freelancers, including how to find freelance work, craft a strong personal brand, write winning proposals, provide great customer service, and manage the logistical aspects of being a "business of one". Roughly a third of trainees continue to freelance – as cleaners, photographers, Uber drivers, or IT support staff. Some realise that freelancing can also be a ladder to the career they want and to secure a conventional full-time job.

Like Kristopher, a former fitness trainer, who used the freelancing skills he learned at Samaschool to change careers. He began performing IT gig work on digital platforms until he was so good a client offered him a full-time job as a tech analyst.

Those were the days my friend.
We thought they'd never end.
—Mary Hopkin

Chapter 7

Financial security: From cushioned care to building your own armour

There was a time, not long ago, when people had a clear idea about when and how to retire. You reached a certain age, an exit door from working life magically opened in front of you, and once beyond it you could lean back and enjoy the fruits of having carried out your job for decades.

> Those were the days my friend
> We thought they'd never end
> We'd sing and dance forever and a day.

When this song came out in 1968, sung by a blond and starry-eyed Welsh girl, its refrain summed up the optimism that buoyed the baby boomer generation.

> We'd live the life we choose
> We'd fight and never lose
> For we were young
> and sure to have our way.

The future seemed completely welcoming back then.

Women were wearing miniskirts in hippie colours. Economies were expanding. Investment returns were high and demographic trends favourable for the healthy functioning of social security systems in many Western countries.

No doubt there have always been large differences in the way governments around the world protect the welfare of their citizens. Today, some fund their people's basic pension and healthcare needs with taxpayer money, while others rely on regular contributions by employers and workers.

Still, both systems rest on the same pillar. Legions of standard employees in standard bread-and-butter jobs support a much smaller group of people in need (the sick, the old, and the unemployed) with their taxes or social security payments. This was the case when the song of flower power child Mary Hopkin stormed the British charts in the late 1960s.

THE END OF CUSHIONED CARE

Our parents never had much reason to worry about social security. It cushioned their lives, whether they needed a doctor's visit or a pension. An entire generation of Germans, for example, got used to receiving more than paying in. The system magically took care of them. This hard-earned privilege, won by the labour rights movement after years of worker exploitation, became easier and easier to take for granted the longer it was available.

In many countries, social security systems grew rampant over the years, with politicians handing out perks for all sorts of professions and voter groups. But the benefits became increasingly difficult to finance. People started living longer and had fewer children than the baby boomers. But they demanded more, and more expensive, care in old age.

Pension and healthcare costs in advanced economies are now rising so fast that they'll be unaffordable by mid-century without reform, according to OECD projections. Since 1990, public healthcare spending has been increasing faster than overall economic growth in the developed world.[1]

Governments have ratcheted up their borrowing to cover the shortfall. The average public debt in 18 of the world's most advanced economies doubled from 40 to over 80 per cent of GDP between 1980 and 1995, according to the Bank for International Settlements.

The Global Financial Crisis exposed years of excess. Cracks appeared in the social security architecture of many Western countries.

Cash-strapped Greece angered its European neighbours at the height of its debt crisis in 2010 when it struggled to cut back a jungle of unbridled early retirement rules. The general retirement age in Greece is 65, as in many other EU countries. However, Greek trombone players and pastry chefs could start collecting pensions on their 50th birthdays, on the rationale that their work causes them late career breathing problems. Hairdressers enjoyed the same privilege due to the dyes and other chemicals they rub into people's scalps, according to media reports.[2]

In Spain, policemen and miners, singers and dancers could retire when they turned 60. Bullfighters got to hang up their capes at 55.

The issue spread well beyond the so-called PIIGS (Portugal, Italy, Ireland, Greece and Spain), the nations hardest hit by the crisis. From France to Poland, several European countries have come under pressure to curb generous pension rules. In Austria, the average railway employee retired at 53 in 2013.[3] Auditors keep attacking the government for not making enough cuts.

The cushioned social security system of the past is in trouble and Mary Hopkin's song, that ode to nostalgia, now seems more fitting than ever: *Those were the days my friend, we thought they'd never end.* They have ended. The carefree times of comprehensive, state-funded health and pensions are gone. We have to get used to working longer and receiving less in retirement. Public healthcare systems are at the brink of collapse from Britain to Greece.

The changing world of work creates additional headaches for governments because people in atypical employment often have patchy, less predictable earnings and are at greater risk of becoming welfare-dependent.

"FOR MY GENERATION THERE IS NO SAFE PENSION"

In the gig economy, companies deliberately hire "independent workers" to save on social security costs. This tactic shrinks the flow of public pension contributions: it's harder and harder to believe we can count on public social security to sustain us through prolonged periods of unemployment, sickness and old age without surrendering our standard of living.

Neither can we count on companies to fill the void because the fast-growing gig and freelance economy is cutting off workers from corporate schemes that contribute to pension plans and offer all sorts of additional employee benefits (think paid parental leave, dental insurance, free gym pass and meditation classes).

In the liquid life, more and more workers are forced to rely on private insurance to meet their social security needs. It's an uncomfortable situation, and many young people are resigned to the fact that the fat years lie behind them and future is gloomy.

***

Take Arnaud Dallière, a 34-year-old Frenchman from Aix-en-Provence who has been travelling the world since finishing his studies in Entrepreneurship and Marketing at Nancy Business School. Arnaud lived in London, in Sydney, in Barcelona. He moved to New Zealand, back to France, to the Canary Islands and back to Australia. In his wake: a string of short-term jobs and unfulfilled startup dreams.

His stop-start career includes casual gigs in restaurants and clothing shops, a failed yet passionate attempt to set up a business selling Moroccan beach towels, and a brief cooking course. Arnaud is restless. Three days into his latest position as marketing manager at an English language school in Sydney he is already tossing up the next move. He is longing to be his own boss, but hasn't yet figured out how.

Savings? Just enough to pay for the next flight. "If I wanted to save, I would need to travel less, but I don't want to give up travelling," says Arnaud, who owns little more than a suitcase, a surfboard and a laptop. He is sharing a rental apartment with his girlfriend. When he needs a car, he uses Uber or the local car sharing scheme. He has no retirement plan.

"You only think about your pension when you believe in your future. My generation knows there is no safe pension," says Arnaud. He says he tries not to overthink. He tries to live in the now.

***

It may not be the most reasonable attitude, but it mirrors the mindset of millions of young people globally. On the backbench of a rusty four-wheel-drive, a surf instructor from a small town in southern Portugal – one of Vera's friends – recently cracked up laughing. "Pension? Me? I'm 30!" In his last job in a surf school on the Algarve he earned 1,200 euros a month, half of which his boss gave him cash in hand.

It's a common practice in hospitality, tourism and other services industries: employers declare only a fraction of the salaries they pay to lessen their tax and social security burden, leaving employees to figure out on their own how to put enough money aside for retirement. And they need to. The minimum state pension in Portugal amounts to some 250 euros per month for employees who contributed at least 15 years to the system.[4] The government just raised the official pension age to 66.

"Forget it," Vera's friend said. "I'm sure we're all going to work until we die."

BUILDING OUR OWN ARMOUR

We need to step up and take responsibility for our own social security. The future may appear gloomy because the old institutions that used to provide a strong safety net for the baby boomer generation are failing today's youths. Still, there are plenty of reasons to be optimistic because the entire money-making and money-saving industry is changing in ways never thought possible a few decades ago, thanks to automation and digital technology.

Everywhere around the globe firms are popping up that redesign the way we think about pension, health insurance and investment. Many are fast-moving startups, founded by young, tech-savvy people who are fed up with the status quo and eager to make investing fun, cheap, easy and accessible for everyone.

In a massive shake-up of traditional industry practices, these new firms use smartphones, algorithms, chatbots and social media to help people like Arnaud put money aside and stay afloat in precarious, fast-shifting times. They prove that the Flow Generation can thrive even without the strong hand of the government or the expensive services of big bank advisors to create a financial cushion.

We don't even need a particularly large or steady income to take control of our finances.

Wearing funky names such as Plum, Nutmeg or Moneyfarm, many of these startups stand for a new mentality that encourages us to don a farmer's hat and start growing money ourselves – with the help of artificial intelligence, which can now nudge you like a friend to do the right thing.

Firms like Friendsurance and Lemonade, show that we're not alone in a world of failing institutions. These firms harness the power of the internet to shepherd like-minded people together and revive the original model of insurance, with community spirit and solidarity as cornerstones.

The swift expansion of the gig economy has opened up a whole new market for alternative social security services. Recognising the need to provide a new form of safety net for freelancers and gig workers, several digital platforms have launched their own insurance products in partnership with traditional players.

For example, Airtasker collaborates with insurance startup Roobyx (with Lloyd's as underwriter) to protect participants against income loss in case of work injury. It's tailored this offering to the unpredictable working life of freelancers and mini-entrepreneurs, with premiums and benefits that "go up and down each week

in line with your earnings".[5] Ridesharing platform Uber
– still reeling under allegations of worker exploitation –
is now offering free insurance for some drivers.[6]

In the US, the former director of the Freelancers
Union has launched a digital savings platform called
Trupo for the growing number of freelancers and self-
employed people who are slipping out of traditional
safety nets due to the sporadic nature of their work.
Trupo offers them short-term disability insurance,
which covers income loss after injury or sickness.

Need sparks ingenuity – and progress. Yes, there are
solutions! While no magic wand can fully replace the
cushioned care our parents once enjoyed, the current
wave of digital disruption offers us fascinating ways to
save more and pay less for our long-term social security.
Our opportunities will only get brighter as the technologies transforming the financial industry become cheaper
and easier to use.

Governments may succeed in repairing some of the
broken safety nets, but times have fundamentally
changed and we need to do more than shrug off reality
with a resigned "whatever" mindset. It's time to jump
into action and consider three simple principles that will
help us build our personal safety raft for the liquid life.
Think of them as a cheat sheet to guide the Flow
Generation into the future. To be successful in the age of
self-managed social security, we should dare to:

- **Squeeze the middleman** to cut fees. The new money
  managers are robo-advisors and automated investment
  products that we can mix and match at a mouse click.
- **Trust machine nudges** to control our spending habits and
  help us save money when we go shopping, manage our
  bills and sign up for insurances.

- **Join the bandwagon** of like-minded people in new grassroots insurance models who offer to secure our health or protect our assets on better terms than traditional players.

Squeeze the middleman

We need to talk about money. Boring? There's no way around it.

We live in times of growing job uncertainty and dimming pension prospects and we need to figure out how to sustain ourselves not just today, but in years to come. Let's take stock of the situation.

Many of us face pressure to privately supplement our existing public pension options, but it's no easy task because investment markets have become so shaky and murky. Even if we have enough money to set aside for rainy days and old age, we have to wonder how we can make our savings work best for us. Which expert should we call when times get so rocky that they overwhelm the experts themselves?

Markets are still recovering from the widespread misconduct and fraud that led to the Global Financial Crisis and tarred the reputation of an entire industry. A recent GfK poll ranked bankers as least trusted professionals worldwide, and the distrust ran especially high in Europe.[7]

The public image of traders is similarly stained. When it comes to honesty and ethical behaviour, stockbrokers fare just a tad better than salespeople and telemarketers, a new Gallup poll shows.[8]

Regulators have tried to restore trust and order by slapping fines on some of the world's largest banks. Judges sent rogue traders to jail. Governments tightened banking rules. And central banks, in an effort to stabilise the global economy and stimulate growth, pulled out an arsenal of unconventional policies that investors and their advisors are still trying to decipher.

Negative interest rates – in which banks charge you to hold your money – are punishing savers in Switzerland, Sweden, Denmark and Japan. Stock markets remain volatile. Government bonds, traditionally viewed as a safe haven, are now seen as risky.

The old ways of investing and saving for the future have obviously stopped working, and even seasoned financial experts are scrambling for ideas in this strange new era.

It's only fair to ask what we get in return when we pay someone to multiply our money for us. If we're clever, we can lower two kinds of costs that experts charge for handling our investments. First, there are the custodians of our pension money, the fund managers. They charge a commission for finding the safest and most profitable home for our dough.

Second, there are the financial advisors. They sit somewhat on the sides of the financial arena – like football players on the reserve bench who know all the rules of the game, but only jump in when the coach whistles. Financial advisors promise to handle all our money needs for us, from analysing our insurance needs to picking the best pension fund. They too charge fees.

Let's see if we can squeeze both these middlemen to make our pension money go further.

LET MONKEYS BEAT YOUR FUND MANAGER

"Any monkey can beat the market," *Forbes* magazine told readers in 2012. No joke. Several studies have cast doubt on the ability of expert stock pickers to make winning portfolio choices. Luck seems to play a greater role than the pros may want to admit.

When American economist Burton Malkiel claimed in his 1973 bestseller *A Random Walk Down Wall Street* that "a blindfolded monkey throwing darts at a newspaper's financial pages could select a portfolio that would do just as well as one carefully selected by experts", many investors took issue. Some researchers also contested his prediction, but not in a negative way. They thought that Malkiel's claim was too modest.

In a string of experiments, in which computers simulated dart-throwing monkeys, researchers proved that blindfolded simians may not only beat human investors, but also outperform markets.

For example, researchers at California-based investment strategy firm Research Affiliates aped Malkiel's monkeys by letting an algorithm build 100 portfolios, each comprising 30 randomly picked and equally weighted stocks from the largest companies on Wall Street. The surprising result: over an almost 50-year period from 1964 to 2010, the monkeys beat the market in more than 9 cases out of 10.

Another study, done by a clever *MarketWatch* columnist, shows that the monkeys win even when pitched against hedge fund managers, who pride themselves on being the smartest guys on the Street.[9] Hedge funds typically invest in sophisticated portfolios comprising stocks, bonds, cash and all sorts of other complex financial products that promise high returns. They charge serious money for their services – as much as 20 per cent of any profits, on top of a basic fee of 2 per cent of the invested assets, according to *MarketWatch*.

Yet the research shows that the dumbest portfolios consisting of a savings account at your local bank and a collection of stocks picked by the monkey produced bigger returns than the hedge fund geniuses year after year after year, even when the monkey is instructed to keep the same risk levels.[10]

Ordinary pension funds, unlike hedge funds, are typically low-risk, low-fee investments, designed to produce decent returns while also preserving the capital of retirees for as long as possible. Yet they too slip money from your wallet.

On average, twelve out of every thousand dollars (or 1.2 per cent) invested in an ordinary mutual fund end up in the pockets of its manager every year, according to US data.[11] This rate is also common among mutual fund managers in other developed countries, who usually charge a basic management fee of 1 to 2 per cent. The slice may seem small, but it adds up. After 30 years you will have paid around 40 per cent of your initial investment just in fees.

No doubt, successful fund managers deserve rewards, and most people are happy to pay someone who understands the labyrinth of financial markets and knows how to diversify portfolios and hedge against risks. But what's the point of a fund manager if a machine – or a monkey – can also get it right?

Automated investment products are beginning to conquer the financial industry. Many of these new, algorithmic options produce returns that are just as solid or even superior to those of human money managers and advisors – while costing only a fraction of the fees and commissions.

Take some of the most passive, most standard and most foolproof asset classes on the market: exchange-traded funds, or ETFs. They've become one of the most popular investment types in recent years because they

charge fees as little as 0.07 per cent.[12] They cost so little because they don't think or behave like a fund manager who typically follows an "active investment strategy", which is a fancy term for being picky about when, where and what to sell.
Many ETFs are not.
They just sit there, mirroring the returns of an entire stock group.
There are ETFs for every investor taste, theme and trading area. Some ETFs comprise only gold stocks or tech stocks or Chinese startups or South American mining stocks. Some invest in bonds, others buy all available stocks in a market, no picking required.

For example, the SPDR SPY S&P500 (in trader speak this mouthful of an acronym becomes the "spider spy") tracks the performance of the US stock index comprising the 500 largest companies on Wall Street.

ETFs are one way to squeeze the first middleman, the fund manager. People trade ETFs like stocks on major exchanges, and any mom-and-pop investor can buy them with a click from any e-banking website. These funds suit the Flow Generation's need to assemble a cheap pension portfolio without much fuss. They just stack them together like Lego blocks until they have built their own diversified portfolio without having to join a more expensive mutual fund.

If you don't know what an active investment strategy is, consider buying ETFs. You can do it yourself or ask an advisor to help you. Or you get a robot to do it.

LET THE ROBO DO THE PENSION JOB

As if! As if a 25-year old girl from London would just walk up to the bank clerk with the fake smile and grey suit and ask about investing. Daniella Camilleri's face lights up from laughing. "Seriously, imagine the conversation!" she says. "Good morning, I would like to start investing. I have about 100 quid. What would the bank say, other than 'Go away'?" Investing sounds scary. That's what Daniella always thought. In her head investing was reserved for middle-aged men with big wallets, big cars and big stacks of credit cards. Not for a girl her age who works in a startup and lives in a shared apartment.

At home, money was always a topic, but investing was not. Her parents split up when she was a baby, and Daniella, raised by her single mum in London, learned to be resourceful.

"I'm good with money," she would say even years later when, as a young urban professional, she would habitually skip takeaway coffees and bring homemade lunch to work to save money.

This year, however, a robot called Plum changed her mind. The machine monitors her bank account, tracks her spending patterns and puts aside a few pounds here and there before Daniella even notices. The bot invests Daniella's savings – no matter how big or small – in mutual funds and ETFs.

It chats with her, like a friend, via Facebook Messenger. No awkward silence as in a bank lobby, no financial jargon, no investment angst. It simply diverts the money out of sight and into an investment fund before Daniella can spend it on something unnecessary.

In the first month, Plum saved her 60 pounds.

***

Firms like Plum are part of the growing universe of "robo-advisors". No, it's not the title of a futuristic Arnold Schwarzenegger film. Robo-advisors are the new superstars in portfolio management. They are computer programs that help humans invest money.

Imagine robo-advisors as the new middlemen between financial markets and our savings. They assess our investment goals, check our risk tolerance and make a few recommendations. If we agree, these machines automatically select the most suitable investment products and build a personalised portfolio we can access online or with an app. Algorithms handle all the trading while making sure the portfolio stays within our comfort zone for risk. Some bots even know how to reduce our tax bill by making clever portfolio moves.

No wonder automated portfolio managers are spreading fast. There is Moneyfarm in Italy and the UK, Betterment in the US and Stockspot in Australia. In Germany alone, investors can choose from more than 20 different robo-advisors, according to research by newspaper *Die Zeit*. Some come from young, upstart firms like Vaamo or Scalable Capital. Others bear the stamp of traditional banks which – like the universities that have changed their curricula to bite-sized online courses – realise they will lose market share if they don't adapt to the Flow Generation's needs.

This generation of investment customers wants to do all its banking via smartphone and may only have peanuts, rather than thousands of dollars, to stow away. Robo-advisors are listening. They don't wear suits, they charge little and they happily take on peanut investments.

Vaamo, the German robo-advisor with a preference for ETFs, starts accounts from as little as 10 euros. Its app shows users exactly how far away their investments are from their retirement goals. Wealthfront, one of the largest robo-advisors in the US, opens accounts from

$500 and charges 0.25 per cent per year.[13] An average human financial advisor requires four to eight times as much, often on top of a starting fee to draft an individual financial plan.

Robo-advisors are the trusted money assistants for the Flow Generation. They let us squeeze out the second middleman when we invest our pension savings.

Moneyfarm calculates that by squeezing both – shifting from mutual funds to ETFs and human financial advisors to robo-advisors – an average investor could save half their annual fees.

Many robo-advisors maximise savings by radically trimming all fees and commissions and excess costs from a portfolio. They work brilliantly for someone like Daniella, a first-time investor looking for an easy and affordable way to start her pension fund. They may not be go-to tools for sophisticated investors or anyone who still prefers to deal with a human he can ask questions of (or blame if things go wrong).

New York's Betterment, one of the oldest robo-advisory firms, offers a hybrid investing model for those craving the human touch. It charges standard fees of 0.25 per cent of assets per year, but also offers a "premium service" that costs an additional 0.15 per cent per year and gives customers with investments over $100,000 unlimited telephone access to a team of planners.[14]

LET ALGORITHMS PICK YOUR HEALTH INSURANCE

A similar wave of disruption is hitting the insurance industry. Online marketplaces for insurance slash fees by automating the human broker. Websites like Money Super Market, Compare Group and GoCompare list the services and costs of dozens of insurance providers, making it easy for even the most clueless consumer to compare different policies. While not entirely new, these comparison websites are set to play a much greater role in many European countries, as more people try to supplement or replace their failing public health insurances with a private alternative.

You need a guide to cut your way through the complex, opaque market for private insurance, whose providers offer a wilderness of fees, extras and exemptions. The guide doesn't need to be a human. We may just as well let the algorithm of a comparison website pick the most suitable policy for us.

An automated comparison tool can save people several hundred dollars in fees per year, according to various research reports, including by the Kaiser Foundation, an American non-profit, and Consumer, a British research firm.

Antonio Gagliardi, co-founder of the online comparison platform CompareEuropeGroup, says many people still shy away from taking their insurance needs into their own hands and researching the best deals themselves or through online brokers.

"People do their homework when buying goods like a fridge, or cell phone, or a TV," says Gagliardi. "For some reason, however, they still don't do as much research when buying financial products, which have a much bigger economic impact on their household."

But in some countries, the Flow Generation's protagonists are getting used to being in charge and managing their own insurance. In the UK, 85 per cent of people with internet access have already used digital comparison tools, according to a report by the Competition and Markets Authority, a British government body.

Being in charge also means we have to remain watchful with algorithmic brokers. Industry insiders warn that online marketplaces offer cheap deals as click-bait only to add costly last-minute extras as customers are about to seal the deal.[15]

Others recommend using online marketplaces only for orientation and then calling the insurance provider to ask for a sweeter deal.

Most comparison websites bar participating insurances from giving discounts on other channels. Still, a journalist working for British newspaper *The Telegraph* managed to get an over-the-phone discount of around 10 per cent in 2011.[16] Maybe it was sheer luck. More likely, however, it was the result of human charm and clever negotiation skills in our heavily automated world.

Trust machine nudges to control your spending

It's great to know that automated portfolio managers and insurance brokers can help us squeeze higher returns out of our savings, but what if we don't have enough money to put aside in the first place?

"You can save. You're just not aware of it," says Plum CEO Victor Troukoudes.

He pushes his beeping smartphone to the end of the long, wooden conference table in a converted industrial loft in London's East End and flips a page in his notebook.

"Here," he says, as his pen fills the paper with equations. "Take out the credit products that cost too much, lower your utility bills, cut out everything where the financial system overcharges you and watch how much you can save."

Plum's robo-advisor does hunt-and-kill on money waste. It automatically signs you up for the cheapest electricity and insurance provider. Or it registers you for direct debit billing when you forgot to do it, to save you late payment fees.

Many of Plum's customers are initially hesitant to let an algorithm take over their bank accounts. However, most drop their concerns as soon as they see the results of an unemotional robo-advisor at work. Each year, the average Plum user gains an extra 1,000 pounds in savings and investments, the startup has calculated. With compound interest over a lifetime, say, 50 years, this could amount to between 50,000 and 200,000 pounds at retirement.

***

Daniella didn't trust the machine at the start. "I'm a control freak," she says. Before she installed the robo-advisor on her smartphone, she used to check her bank account balance every day. She knew exactly how much money she could spend, and in weeks with unexpected expenses – when she had to get the heels of her shoes fixed or buy a birthday present for a friend – she would skip the Friday drinks at the pub. "I thought I could not possibly save more money."

The machine proved her wrong.

Because it moved small amounts of money beyond Daniella's awareness, it forced her to adjust her behaviour subconsciously. "You know when you're at the supermarket and you're tired and you just can't be bothered to buy only what you really need?" Plum's bot nudged Daniella to stop wasting cash.

She still checked her balance frequently, but because it was always a tad lower than it would have been without Plum, she automatically spent less, without knowing exactly when and how. She only noticed her savings were growing – thanks to the robot, which was working tirelessly in the background. A few months after first installing the app, Daniella had saved so much money that she decided to give herself a treat: a weekend away in Iceland with her boyfriend to watch the New Year's fireworks illuminate the cold arctic sky.

***

Artificial intelligence is helping us overcome our desire to spend and shop and live in the now without thinking about tomorrow. We all struggle with it because our brains are wired with two decision-making systems: our reflective brain, which is responsible for longer-term, more deliberative thoughts; and our instinct, which makes quick, almost automatic decisions.

The two often conflict. The automatic system seeks immediate pleasure, whereas the reflective system values short-term sacrifices that lead to larger rewards in the future. Our reflective system may want a chicken tomorrow, while the automatic system wants to eat the egg today.

We hate thinking about our retirement because it seems so far away. We also tend to put off difficult choices.

Plum CEO Victor Troukoudes still remembers his dad's nagging voice: "You need life insurance." That was when Victor was in his twenties. "Dad, I'm busy living my life," he replied. But the words stuck. They eventually inspired Victor to co-found Plum with a friend: a tech startup that makes saving money fun and helps us control our desire for immediate rewards.

Behavioural economist Richard Thaler spent a lifetime analysing how humans make complex decisions and earned a Nobel Prize for his work on "nudges". He found that gentle pushes and little prompts at the right time can drastically improve our decisions about health, wealth and happiness.

The nudge concept has succeeded in public policy all over the world. In Europe and the US, governments boosted the number of organ donors using a simple tweak: instead of asking people to sign up as donors, they changed the rules so that every adult was automatically registered with an option to opt out.

Singaporean electricity companies encourage households to save energy by showing them black on white how much the average person in their area pays for power. The idea: you are much more likely to remember to turn off the lights if you know your neighbour's bill is 10 per cent lower.

Little tricks, large consequences. Academics and startup founders say digital nudges can save retirement in our precarious times. The way we live has changed, so the way we save money needs to change as well.

"Many workers have a highly variable stream of income. We need to make it as easy for these workers to save as it is to spend," says Shlomo Benartzi, another behavioural economist who developed a pioneering digital nudge called Save More Tomorrow, which helped over 15 million Americans increase their savings rate.[17]

These apps go beyond basic robo-advisors, which help you invest your money. They piggybank extra money, again and again, so you have more power to invest. Examples include Moneyfarm, Scalable Capital and Nutmeg in the United Kingdom. Apps like Oval Money, available in Italy and UK, round up every credit card purchase to the nearest dollar, pinching a few cents for your savings account each time you go shopping. You'd be surprised how many cakes you can make with all these crumbs.

Benartzi argues that software which automatically moves pre-defined amounts of money into a savings account is one of the most effective ways to save. "If people have to actively think about saving, then they probably won't do it," says Benartzi.

Trust the machines to nudge you. They know how your brain works and can trick you into doing the right thing just by framing your choices in a different way. You can tell someone he would need to save $150 a month, which sounds daunting. Or you can tell that person to save $5 a day, which amounts to skipping a coffee. It just seems more doable.

Tracking your spending patterns in real time on your smartphone screen can further increase your willingness to save. Benartzi and colleagues tested it with an app that showed users exactly how much they were paying each month in restaurants and bars, on mortgages and their health insurance. Once users could see this information on their mobile screens, their average savings went up by more than 15 per cent.[18]

RUN FOR YOUR MONEY

The insurance industry has also discovered how effectively digital nudges can change our behaviour. Their interest makes sense from a corporate point of view: healthier people need less medical attention and reduce expenses for health insurers.

Several insurance companies have introduced programs that offer discounts to clients who agree to have their fitness measured with Fitbits and other high-tech gadgets from the Internet of Things.

While there are justified privacy concerns around excessive personal data mining, we may as well give insurers the benefit of the doubt and harness this opportunity to lower our fees – and improve our health and wellbeing at the same time.

For example, Vitality, a UK-based private insurer, rewards clients who exercise regularly by lowering their healthcare and life insurance premiums by over 10 per cent per year. It uses wristband trackers to monitor how well participants stick to their fitness regime, whether it's running, cycling, swimming or working out in the gym.[19] More than one million people have already signed up for Vitality's health-conscious program. They can gain further perks, including discounted gym memberships, running shoes and bicycles.[20]

In the US, health insurer UnitedHealthcare Services offers cash rewards for clients who hit fitness targets.[21] Can you do 500 steps in seven minutes, six times a day, at least one hour apart? Or 3,000 steps in 30 minutes? Wearable devices track you, and UnitedHealthcare promises that members who hit all their goals can earn up to $1,095 per year – money they can use to cover out-of-pocket medical or pharmacy expenses. [22]

Some companies have gamified the interface of their tracking devices to keep clients motivated. On the Healthy Virtuoso app, colourful circles track your steps and shifting boxes display increasingly attractive options for those who stay healthier. The more they exercise, the larger the rewards and discounts.

JOIN THE CROWD

It's easy to feel stranded on your own in this brave new world. We know we must sort out our social security needs, but is there anything more unexciting than insurance?

Traditional insurance is dull business. There are fees to be paid to cover for events we'd rather not think

209

about. If they do happen, there's paperwork to be filled out, proofs to be shown and rules to be obeyed before we can get reimbursed.

Critics often scold the traditional insurance sector for being bloated and overly bureaucratic. They accuse the industry of deliberately relying on cumbersome procedures as a self-serving mechanism to protect profits and corporate self-interests.

No one should blame us if we'd rather skip the insurance part.

But wait!

Several startups are breathing new life into this sleep-inducing realm. Harnessing digital technology, these so-called peer-to-peer insurance firms offer a rescue raft to the Flow Generation. They reassure us that we're not on our own in a world of failing institutions and greedy corporations. In contrary, we can get by with a little help from our friends (to echo the Beatles), and once we start relying on our trusted networks, we even pay a lot less to insure the risks we face in life.

Peer-to-peer (P2P) models are revolutionising insurance. They apply the principles of social networking to this sector, and Berlin-based startup Friendsurance is arguably the movement's pioneer. It all started in 2010, when Tim Kunde, a former management consultant, sat down with a bunch of friends to put a question mark behind everything they knew about insurance. What if, they thought, we could organise insurance like a Facebook community? Wouldn't that reduce the friction between insurance companies and beneficiaries? Wouldn't that increase trust, transparency and goodwill? And bring down costs?

Shoddy claims are the biggest cost drivers in insurance. They tend to rise as insurance pools grow. It's an issue of trust and incentives that economists call "moral hazard".

There are ways to keep this hazard low. Research shows that people behave more honestly when insured in smaller groups of peers with similar risk profiles. A report by SwissRe, one of the world's largest insurance groups, shows that keeping insurance circles small can lower claim costs by over one quarter compared to the industry average.[23] Less fraud, lower claim costs, better rates for everyone.

Development aid workers have known this for years. When they travel to impoverished villages in Africa, India or the South Pacific to hand out microloans, they find their financial impact is greatest when credit risks are spread across fewer heads.

Muhammad Yunus, a Bangladeshi social entrepreneur and economist, first harnessed the power of peer pressure in finance. In the early 1980s, he launched Grameen Bank, a pioneer social project also known as "Bank of the Poor", which earned Yunus the Nobel Prize for Peace. Before Grameen Bank handed out microcredit to the poorest of the poor, it asked borrowers to present five references from people in the community (not relatives) to vouch for their ability and intent to repay the loan. The system worked. Grameen Bank soon outperformed other lenders in Bangladesh.

The mechanics of peer groups appealed to Tim Kunde and his friends. Friendsurance, the startup Kunde co-founded, revives the concept of insurance as a solidarity community, in which a small circle of peers keeps each other honest. They are an intermediary, yes, but the approach is quite an innovative one and it saves people a lot of money. Here's how it works: customers still buy a traditional insurance, but Friendsurance makes sure they get better conditions. The firm steps in as a broker for people who are happy to accept a higher excess – the out-of-pocket expense members pay in the event of a claim – in return for lower premiums.

The trick: Friendsurance members don't keep the savings from lower premiums in their own wallets, they agree to pay them into a shared pool, which acts like a piggybank for rainy day events. When members do need to make a claim, the piggybank covers the excess, sparing them from having to pay individual out-of-pocket expenses.

Still, the incentive to avoid claims is strong. If money remains in the pool at the end of the year, each member gets some cash back. If no one makes a claim, they can retrieve as much as 40 per cent of their premiums. In the event that too many claims have arisen and the money in the pool is not enough, a kind of "reinsurance" becomes effective.

Today, Friendsurance has grown to more than 150,000 members, but the startup deliberately keeps a lid on its insurance groups. Ten people are part of an average group, just enough to evoke the spirit of how villagers looked after each other hundreds of years ago. If one family's house burns down, the others come to the rescue. No questions asked.

Getting rewarded for good behaviour is the biggest difference from traditional insurance companies, which don't usually reimburse members who stay claim-free. US-based peer-to-peer insurance Lemonade is driven by an even bigger social mission: encouraging members to donate leftover pool money to charity.

"Instant everything. Killer prices. Big heart," touts the startup on its website. Savings can be substantial. Lemonade, which focuses on property, insures rental apartments for as little as $5 a month, less than half the average American cost of around $12, according to often-cited industry sources.[24]

The P2P insurance market is still nascent and firms like Friendsurance have so far mostly brokered protection against smaller risks, insuring against bicycle theft, smartphone damage, burglary or legal costs.

However, the newcomers are gaining ground and are slowly moving into more complex and competitive markets. An American startup called Oscar Health Insurance offers P2P products in this space, and Huddle has similar ones for travel and cars.

While traditional insurance companies treasure red tape and time-consuming paper trails, P2P startups move at the speed of a mouse click to get members the cheapest deal.

Like robo-advisory firms, they offer their services through smartphone apps and AI chatbots. They also use social media to connect like-minded people who are looking for insurance that is affordable, transparent and easy to understand.

These small, social P2P insurance firms speak the language of the Flow Generation.

"Hey, I'm Maya. I'll get you an awesome price in seconds. Ready to go?"

The face of Lemonade's chatbot looks a bit like Heidi Klum: blond, blue-eyed, big smile. Who wouldn't want to talk about home insurance with her? About anything, really. Maya looks like the smart best friend you always wanted at school to explain the fundamental theorems of calculus. She looks like she can turn even the most boring topic into fun and games.

"Let's do this!" Maya quips.

We're hooked. Absolutely. "Let's do this, Maya."

For once, insurance seems like something we can manage, and P2P startups do everything they can to keep us engaged. Some post short animated video clips to help even the most financially illiterate person understand their business model. Others, like Teambrella, a peer-to-peer insurance with pilot teams in the USA, Argentina, Peru, Russia, Germany and the Netherlands, give members full control over the cash pots they feed with their premiums.[25]

A novelty in the insurance world, Teambrella is entirely based on teamwork: people with the same insurance needs – whether it's covering the risk of a car accident or smartphone theft – band together. When one member makes a claim, the group comes together to discuss the matter and decides, by online vote, how much the payout should be. In the end, everyone chips in to settle the claim.

It's the villager model of extinguishing a fire.

Teambrella is a crowd-managed alternative to the big corporate model of insurance, although its business model – based on peace, harmony and fair debate among small groups of people willing to look after each other – may never reach scale.

Still, some P2P insurers have discovered a new frontier. They want to make the Flow Generation's life even easier by becoming a robo-supported one-stop-shop for all sorts of insurance needs.

Friendsurance is already offering a service that involves screening a client's current policies and seeing if cheaper products are available elsewhere. London-based robo-advisor Plum is doing the same for financial products. Both firms use software to scour markets.

Their move is a blow to the insurance industry's middlemen, those brokers who typically have incentive to sell us new products rather than screening our existing products for value or need.

Imagine a future where our robo-advisor could tell us, just by sifting through our bank account statements, that we need a new employee insurance policy because we've switched to working freelance. The robot might also understand immediately that we had a baby, after detecting regular expenses for nappies on our shopping receipts, and suggest we move to a family insurance.

It sounds futuristic, but this future is not far away.

I'm just an animal looking for a home
and share the same space
for a minute or two.
— Talking Heads

Chapter 8

Living space: From "My home is my castle" to "My home is my hostel"

The ice cubes have melted into a puddle at the bottom of Nicoló's cocktail glass. It's the golden hour in Mykonos, when the harsh Greek sun fades to a gentle glow and the seaside tables fill with the chatter of sometimes silly, sometimes serious reflections on life.

"Another round before sunset?"

Nicoló and his friends have been sitting here for a while. They watch the tourists stroll past in their summer dresses and the yachtsmen anchor their big white sailing boats in the bay. What would it be like, they ask, to win the lottery? How would you spend your money?

Would you impress more girls if you owned a Ferretti boat or a Ferrari car? What about the people you'd attract with all this bling: would you really want to be with them? And if owning property is so important, how come none of us has had the guts or wealth to buy at least an apartment?

The waiter brings the bill before they can finish their thoughts. The scooters start with a sputter, but then they hum over the winding roads, back home to the small holiday apartments they have rented for a week. There's no point in continuing the conversation. The helmets swallow all sounds, the wind carries away all words, but the questions remain in Nicoló's head as he rides through the dry Aegean summer.

***

In the past, it seemed a life achievement to own a house, a car, a boat. Material wealth promised social recognition and financial independence. Today, however, the grand goal of exclusive ownership is fading.

House prices across the developed world have reached Himalayan heights and fewer and fewer people can afford them. Steady jobs are in decline and wage growth is stagnant, which makes it harder to save money. In the United Kingdom, a brutal housing shortage has seen house prices rise six times faster than wages in recent years.[1] In San Francisco, Los Angeles and several other large American cities, the average young person now needs at least a decade to put aside enough for a 20 per cent down payment on an apartment.[2]

Loans are also harder to get, and to finance, as banks are less willing to lend to freelancers or anyone else with low savings and shaky income prospects.

Priced out of the housing market, the share of young adults still living at home continues to rise from Canada to Ireland.[3] In Italy, these youths are (often unfairly) mocked as *bamboccioni,* "overgrown babies," unable to build their own nest. Almost 90 per cent of the country's people between 16 and 29 still live with their parents – one of the highest rates in the EU.[4] Many can't afford rentals either, as those costs have also soared while income prospects remain dim. If renting is impossible, then owning a house has clearly become a distant dream for an entire generation of youths.

But here's the good news: the rise of the data and platform economy, with its proliferation of sharing models and financial technology startups, is inviting us to take a fresh look at the former must-haves in life.

Members of the Flow Generation aren't wedded to the life goals of their forebears, who dreamed of picket fences and glitzy show-off symbols. Rather, they have begun to harness some wildly unconventional financing and housing options that fit their fluid, cash-strapped existence.

We know that the growing love for collective consumption is boosting house and car sharing platforms, such as Airbnb and Uber. What's new is that the sharing phenomenon is now reaching into the far remote corners of our economy, where mortgage lenders and property developers preside over spreadsheets full of percentage points and interest rate calculations.

In the shadows of big banks that used to decide whether we could ever buy property, hip fintechs have begun to flourish. These startups are coming to our rescue, as we redefine what it means to call a place or thing "our own" in a world of skyrocketing property prices and increasingly nomadic work.

Firms such as BrickX, HomeFundIt, and Loftium show that we don't have to give up our dream of becoming a homeowner. We only need to reimagine it.

Who would have thought that today's cleverest property investors would be perfectly happy to own just a few bricks worth of an inner-city apartment? New co-financing models make it possible. Young people from

Manhattan to Malmö now scour their social networks for the starting capital to buy a home – through crowdfunding platforms or peer-to-peer lenders.

And where previous generations used to say, "My home is my castle", the Flow Generation's pioneers now proudly proclaim, "My home is a hostel" – thanks to fintechs that help cash-strapped home buyers scramble together enough money for a mortgage deposit if they, in turn, agree to rent out bedrooms on Airbnb and share the proceeds.

All these creative new financing options have one goal: making property ownership more affordable and fun. They complement a range of more traditional co-living arrangements which are experiencing a renaissance among modern hipsters: funky urban share houses with communal washing machines. Or rural land co-operatives with enough space to build your personal dream home.

The following pages explore the new, colourful, even revolutionary ways to build our own nest in the liquid life. First, however, we need to examine our mindset.

Speak bluntly with yourself

It's time to ask tough questions: Do we really need to buy a house, and why? Are we just afraid of missing out on a property bonanza that seems to be making everyone else rich but us? Whose storyline are we living when we claim we want to own a house? Is it really ours? That of our parents? Of our culture? Can we reset our priorities from ownership to access, from hoarding treasures to sharing services?

Buyers can behave like drug addicts. Several neuroscientists have proved in brain experiments that shopping triggers a rush of dopamine in our bodies, which is the chemical stuff that gives us a feeling of bliss. Many consumers no longer shop because they need something, according to research commissioned by Greenpeace.[5] They shop because they like shopping.

Our emotional affair with buying extends beyond clothes and shoes and electronic gadgets. For many people, a house purchase is more about feeling than rationality. Over half (56%) of British homeowners said in 2016 they made an offer on their current or previous home simply because they "fell in love with it", according to a survey by My Home Move, a service that helps people buy, sell and re-mortgage houses.[6]

However, the high can fade as quickly as it arose and leave shoppers, like alcoholics, feeling intense guilt. Every second person Greenpeace surveyed in Europe and Asia confessed that the buzz from shopping wears off within a day. After the binge the hangover.

With homes, the high can turn into a nightmare. Two out of three young Americans under 35 told the latest Bank of the West Millennial Study that they regretted buying a home and wished they had been more prepared going into the purchase. Some 44 per cent said that once they inked the deal, they felt stuck in one place, found damage in the house or discovered that the space didn't work for their family. Two out of five cited budgetary regrets, saying they felt stretched too thin.[7]

Too often logic only whispers when it comes to home buying. A house is both a cocoon and a prestige object, a symbol of prosperity and status, of wealth and power, often passed down over generations. Many people attach part of their personality to the home. Moving away from it can be a deeply emotional experience.

Owning the roof over your head signals "respectability, seriousness of purpose, and a willingness to settle down and become a productive community member", argues Israeli academic Avital Margalit. In Israel, she says, people cherish homes as their most valuable possessions – economically, socially and psychologically.[8]

Her observation applies to many other countries. Home possession is a fixture in the "American dream". The same applies to Australia, where owning a backyard with a barbecue proclaims success in life. During Italy's "economic miracle" after the Second World War, the building boom that went hand in hand with economic recovery would have been unthinkable if home ownership weren't a status symbol.

Having your own house also promises the ultimate financial security. At some point, we hope, our house will become our life raft for retirement, so we can stop working and at least not have to pay rent anymore. Housing markets may have crashed around the world, but we still view "brick and mortar" as one of the best and safest long-term investments we can make. Germans affectionately refer to real estate as *Betongold*: concrete gold.

It's easy to see why so many people worry that home ownership has moved beyond their reach. But is this widespread frustration justified?

From a purely financial point of view, buying a house is not necessarily the best investment choice. Sure, according to popular belief and the wisdom of our (grand)fathers, brick and mortar have indestructible value. But some clever young guns on Wall Street know that if we merely want solid long-term returns, we can do better with our money.

Not long ago, a financial advisor named Chris Reining earned accolades with investment tactics that made him a millionaire at the age of 35. Reining is a fan of index funds, not property. And he turned to data collected by US Nobel Laureate Robert Shiller to debunk the myth that real estate is a superior long-term investment to stocks.

He tracked the performance of US housing markets over more than 125 years, starting in 1890, and then compared it with the growth of America's stock market in different decades. The surprise result: in an average year and adjusted for inflation, a property buyer would have gained 0.39 per cent on his investment. Had he bought the share index S&P500 instead, he would have earned 6.48 per cent in an average year.[9]

British researchers came to the same eye-opening conclusion: equities, not housing, make for the most profitable long-term investment. This is partly due to the higher risk investors shoulder when investing in equity. However, "claims that housing provides a large financial reward at lower risk are incorrect," says the team of researchers from Credit Suisse and the London Business School.[10]

Our lives are changing fast and we should ask ourselves whether home prices up in oxygen-mask territory are really worth the social recognition, the pleasure and the pride we may get from such a long-term investment. We may pay an irrational premium just to experience the buzz of imprinting our name on a house that might outlast us, like an old tree whose bark still wears the carved initials of childhood friends who once longed to be sweethearts forever.

Honestly, we should think twice – and maybe more – before we jump on the buyer bandwagon.

Once we are clear about our motivation, we can sift through the available solutions. Because there are solutions for anyone open-minded about property.

A fast-growing universe of fintech startups supports whichever living and housing scenario we feel most comfortable with, even if we don't have a full-time job or six-digit savings. Some of these startups exist only in certain cities or countries, and others are still in their infancy. However, they remind us that we need to be more creative, adaptable and entrepreneurial today to achieve our dreams – whether we are making small decisions or big ones, such as changing jobs or buying homes.

The old norms aren't valid in the liquid life. The Flow Generation's pioneers have already freed themselves from old-fashioned ideas about what homeowners look like, and how they should behave, and they feel free to:

- Rent.
- Own bricks, not buildings.
- Buy in teams.
- Borrow creatively.
- Join a modern housing community.

RENT: THROW AWAY THE MORTGAGE ANCHOR

What's wrong with renting?

Some people are completely comfortable with the idea of never buying property. Ever. Part of it is cultural. The country we live in clearly influences whether we keep dreaming the homeowner's dream. Renting may sound far-fetched in a country like Romania or Singapore, where over 90 per cent of the population owns a home. But fly to Austria or Switzerland and you'll find a strong rental culture. In Germany, close to 50 per cent of all homes are rented, the highest rate in the EU.[11]

Part of it is generational. Things are shifting on a massive scale and across borders. The Flow Generation is getting used to the rental market as their parents never did. Look at the United Kingdom. There, home ownership among 25- to 34-year-olds with a decent middle income has collapsed from 65 per cent to 27 per cent over the past twenty years, according to the Institute for Fiscal Studies, a British think tank.[12] Home ownership, once the norm, is not even common.

Priced out of the buyer's game, more and more young adults around the world are making a virtue out of necessity. They are nomadic workers or urban digital natives with volatile freelance incomes, who are only too glad to escape the hassle and financial pressure of owning an asset and carrying a mortgage on their backs – as long as they can still access the same asset through the booming sharing and on-demand economy.

Ownership is overrated when access is all you need.

Around one in 10 young Americans expect to rent for the rest of their lives, and that share is on the rise, according to a recent survey of thousands of Millennials by real estate portal Apartment List.[13]

Sure, most of those surveyed still aspire to buy a house sometime in the future, and many are upset that they can't save enough money for down payments. However, (surprisingly?) many also say they prefer to stay uncommitted and free – at least for now. One third declare they aren't ready to settle down yet and over one quarter say they want to get married first.

The same story unfolds in the UK, where young adults under 35 are increasingly sceptical of homeownership. Of those already tied to mortgages, almost half would advise their peers to continue renting due to falling house prices and higher costs of living, according to a recent survey by Get Living, a property developer. One in five would rather invest their money in cryptocurrencies, such as Bitcoin, with 57 per cent considering property investment a "high risk" over the five years to 2023.[14]

"Contrary to belief we found that not all Millennials are scrambling to get on the property ladder," states the Get Living survey, adding 9 in 10 Brits surveyed see big benefits in renting. "It suits their lifestyle, their life stage and offers them a better living experience."

***

They spent the morning diving in the deep blue off Mykonos, but now the friends are lazing under the beach umbrella, shaking sand out of books and wiping sunscreen fingerprints off smartphones. "Check this out! For sale!" They bend over the photo on Nicoló's phone display. A balcony overlooking the sea in their Italian home town. "Maybe if I used all my savings and some family money..." Nicoló doesn't finish his thought.

What difference would it make? How many Greek island escapes would he have to give up to pay back the mortgage?

He returns to his holiday read, Tim Ferris' *The 4-Hour Workweek*. The book, a lifestyle bible for millions of freelancers, has made a mark on him. Its core idea: chase experiences, not assets. Own less, live more. The author argues that most people use "dream assets" like sports cars, holiday houses or private jets far less often than they initially imagined and could be better off splashing their money on creative travel adventures to inexpensive countries, where they can use the same goods for a fraction of the ownership costs.

Why not spend five days on a tropical island in Panama where local fishermen share their fresh catch of the day and show you the best dive spots? Ferris did it for $250. On another occasion he spent just $1,200 on a four-week luxury trip that took him from Buenos Aires to Berlin – airfares, penthouse apartments, and five-star restaurants included.

"Maybe I should book a trip to Indonesia instead of buying a house," says Nicoló. His friend, a 29-year-old lawyer, looks at him through his sunglasses. "I would love to move out of my parents' place," he says.

HOMES FOR NOMADS

In 1950, when *Cinderella* was an international box office hit, people paid less than half a dollar for a ticket and a tub of popcorn. Today, even adjusted for inflation, we pay almost twice as much just to see a movie. Although we don't have to. We could sit at home on the couch, switch on a streaming service like Netflix and see anything in a whole film library for the cost of about one movie ticket per month.

Streaming services have significantly lowered the cost of entertainment, and a number of startups are now applying the Netflix model to the property worries of the Flow Generation. These startups use digital technology to offer "homes on demand" – by making living spaces available for just a couple of days or weeks, instead of months or years. It sure suits the nomadic lifestyle and the shifting careers of modern laptop workers.

Renting has its own challenges. Even if we bid farewell to the dream of ever owning a house and are happy to rent, we need to clear some financial hurdles.

Landlords and real estate agencies usually ask tenants to sign a long-term lease of 12 months and pay several months of rent in advance, on top of a security deposit. These rigid requirements can clash with the increasingly jagged careers and unpredictable life paths of the Flow Generation. Many people today are unable, or unwilling, to make long-term plans.

"People's life doesn't fit into 12-month periods anymore", says Flip, an American startup.

Four weeks work experience in Manhattan? Ask Flip to find you the perfect place to sublet. Six months freelancing from Venice Beach? Flip organises the lease and sorts out all paperwork with the landlord. And if you need to get going quickly for whatever reason, the firm lines up a new tenant to take over the lease. It's like Airbnb for the modern on-the-go professional – people who are keen to stay longer than a few days, but never long enough for a traditional rental contract.

London-based startup Reposit helps renters who start sweating at the idea of paying a security deposit of six weeks' worth of rent. With Reposit, tenants just pay for one week in form of a non-refundable fee, which the startup uses to insure landlords against loss from rogue tenants. Tenants pay more only if they break something or forget to hire a cleaner at the end of their lease.

The innovation lies not so much in the technology, but in the finance. Reposit believes that in our smartphone world "property should be let out at lightning speed", just as we stream a Netflix movie for small coin whenever and wherever we want.

RENT OR BUY? ASK AN ALGORITHM

Surfers have a favourite way of making other surfers jealous on days when the ocean is flat and not a single wave lines up on the horizon. "You should have been here yesterday," they say. "Yesterday was pumping."

Renters can feel a similarly remorse these days. "We should have bought five years ago. We'd be rich today," they say. "What did we do instead? We kept renting."

Fear is the fuel of financial markets.

Whether there's a property frenzy, a startup craze, a bitcoin rage or a tulip mania, nobody wants to sit on the sidelines while others rake in fortunes simply because they bought the right asset at the right place and the right time.

House price booms in many parts of the Western world, from Montreal to Munich, have infected millions of people with an uncontrollable fear of missing out (FOMO). Many feel compelled to buy property – not for the love, but for the money.

Renting could still be the better deal. Many homebuyers fork out a substantial premium for their purchase and get it back only after several years, in which they could just as well have rented and invested this chunk of money elsewhere.

Many even know they overpay, but do it nonetheless to get a foot in a market they speculate will continue to rise.

The premium that homebuyers willingly or unknowingly pay depends on many assumptions and costs related to financing, utility and maintenance, as well as present and future market developments.

How much money are we really sacrificing when we think buying is best?

It's easy to get the equation wrong when we have caught the FOMO bug. Time to call the robots for help and rely on the sober maths of an algorithm to solve this classic housing dilemma.

A popular tool is the *New York Times*'s Rent vs Buy Calculator which works for any house in the world. It asks users to estimate how much money they will likely pay each month on mortgage costs, electricity bills, repairs and other fixtures. It crunches the numbers. Then it makes a bold call: "If you can rent a similar home for less than [AMOUNT X], then renting is better." Such calculators also exist for specific countries, including CMDataWeb in Italy and Comprar-Alquilar-Simulador in Spain.

How much house can I afford? Online tools such as SmartAsset and NerdWallet answer this question for American homebuyers after analysing large data piles, including from household income surveys or the fine print of bank loan offerings. British homebuyers can use the *BBC News* House Price Calculator.

Renting or buying? These algorithmic platforms can help us decide. The hardest part might be to enter the correct information and, most importantly, to let our head prevail.

Own bricks, not buildings

Property investing can be a gamble. Even if you think you spotted a sure-fire winner, a cash cow in the form of an apartment or house, you could be wrong. There could be hidden cracks in the walls, or the location could lose its appeal for whatever reason.

Financial markets can behave like a casino, and property markets are no exception. After every boom comes a bust and even savvy investors get burned. So why risk it all on one bet? If the point of buying real estate is investment, we may as well spread our limited savings over several properties, instead of buying just one.

Several fintech startups are helping investors to do just that. They buy a bunch of houses, divvy them up into thousands of small pieces and serve each fraction to a willing buyer for as little as $33 Australian dollars.[15] The startups won't give the investor physical access to the property, but rather the ability to tap into the returns.

The concept, known as "fractional ownership", is becoming popular around the globe – not just among cash-strapped first-time home buyers (who use it as a keyhole entry into a property market that has locked them out), but also among more experienced investors seeking to diversify their real estate portfolios.

Australia, South Africa, the UK and the US have emerged as hotspots for startups in the fractional ownership space.

At BrickX, for example, several hundred people become joint owners of properties ranging from small beachside studios in Sydney to Victorian-style town-houses in Melbourne. Investors can treat the house shares, aptly called "bricks", like company stocks. They can buy and sell fractions of different houses, and assemble them into a personal portfolio with a maximum stake of 5 per cent in each property. Each month, they receive a rental income like landlords. When they sell, they also receive a sliver of their property's increase in value – if there is any.

Investors can jump in and out of the property game whenever they like. However, BrickX charges a fee for buying or selling property stakes, which makes it more attractive to stay invested for the longer term. The British investment platform Brickowner uses a similar model to help investors buy a piece of a house, rather than the whole mansion.

Nowadays we don't even have to be millionaires to own a chunk of luxury property. There's a growing market for high-end fractional property buyers. One such company, Elite Destination Homes, sells stakes of around 10 per cent (or five weeks every year) of fancy apartments in Paris.

Buyers need more than pocket money, though. A stake in a "cute" three-bedroom apartment in the elegant 6th Arrondissement costs $250,000, plus maintenance fees of up to $12,000 per year, according to the firm. Slightly cheaper, but for lesser time: a one-week share in a 600-square-metre penthouse at the Four Seasons Resort on the Caribbean island of Anguilla. A platform called Luxury Fractional Guide offers it for $95,000.

Buy in teams

In continental Europe, startups have been less active in this field. Here, fractional ownership typically follows an older "timeshare" model. Friends or strangers buy houses together which they can then reserve for certain periods each year – either to rent out or to spend their own holidays in them. It might be the perfect solution for the Flow Generation's aspiring property investors: buy in a team, not alone.

What's holding us back? The market is still young. Even in Australia, one of the world's most developed property markets, two out of three people have never even heard of co-ownership, according to Kohab, an online marketplace that acts like dating app Tinder for prospective real estate buyers.[16] The platform matches complete strangers with similar investment preferences and helps them make a joint property purchase. Guiding two (or more) interested buyers through a jumble of legal and financial issues, the platform also removes a huge hindrance to the co-buying trend: legal uncertainty.

Without these hurdles, around one out of four millennials in the United Kingdom would seriously consider buying a house with family, friends or even strangers.[17] Yet many don't get close to these deals, as they see them as messy and full of bureaucracy.

On Kohab, people can pool their savings to qualify for bigger mortgages. They can also use the app's property search function to find the best deals in an area as well as split deal closing costs and down payments. Before people become co-investors, they sign a legal agreement that safeguards their individual interests.

Other companies harness blockchain technology to help strangers team up as trusted homebuyers. The startup Atlant, for example, uses smart contracts that rely on this new technology (and a cryptocurrency like bitcoin) to get co-buying deals done safely and quickly.[18]

While the world of bitcoins and blockchains may sound exotic, it represents one puzzle piece in an exciting new trend: more companies are using easy, smartphone-friendly technologies to change the way we invest in houses – whether we already have enough spare cash or still need to raise it.

No money? No problem: Be a creative borrower

We might be desperate to settle into our own little abode because, well, maybe we're just hopelessly romantic or we're in thrall to an instinct from the caveman era. We dream of buying a family home, not just a house. What if our savings account barely gets us an inner-city garage, let alone a campervan?

Property markets are heated, and most banks are bound to play it safe, with loan schemes that are geared towards the standard employee with a secure standard job and a history of standard monthly payments.

Still, times may appear tougher than they are. Unpredictable circumstances call for unusual solutions. If we dare to venture outside the trodden paths toward home ownership, we will find a growing arsenal of funding alternatives to help us achieve our housing dream, even if we are short on cash.

These creative financing options, hatched from an avant-garde of property-focused fintechs, turn home ownership into a team effort. They encourage us to harness the power of crowds to scramble together a mortgage deposit. "We can call on new models such as co-owning with a lender, peer-to-peer lending, crowdfunding and space-sharing.

Let's have a look. We may not immediately claim full ownership of a place to call home. But we dramatically increase our chances that one day, soon, we will.

HOMESHARE WITH A LENDER

For teachers in sunny California, life recently got a lot easier. Not that they don't have anything to worry about. Their days are packed with classroom routines, boundary-testing children and traffic jams on their way to work. And finding a place to call their own in the expensive San Francisco Bay Area, magnet for the world's largest tech companies, can be draining.

Few public servants can match the fat paychecks of IT executives. However, an initiative called Landed has put the homebuyer's dream back within reach for Californian teachers. The startup (which is backed by venture capitalists, bankers, philanthropists, Stanford economists, and public policy experts) offers teachers and other professionals from an "indispensable segment of society" some starting capital if they agree to hand over a piece of their dream home.

Landed pays up to half the down payment. In return, it asks its beneficiaries to partly share the profit of a future sale – or cover part of any loss, in case the house value drops – after 10 or 30 years depending on the contract terms. The firm now operates in several high-cost US cities, including Denver, Los Angeles, San Francisco and Seattle.

The biggest difference from other fractional owner-ship models like BrickX or Brickowner: Landed's clientele can live in the house they share with their lenders. They can make it their cosy family home, plant tomatoes in the garden and watch their children grow up under its roof.

Point, another such startup based in San Francisco, provides homebuyers with an interest-free loan of up to $250,000 they can put toward a house purchase. Home-owners, in exchange, agree to sell the property at some point and pay the firm a slice of the profit. People with enough money can buy out Point at a later date.

The concept of buying a home by sharing a piece of it with a private lender is still relatively new. In Europe, it's hard to find startups that grant fractional owners the right to live in their investment properties. However, since some of the world's brainiest trends and innova-tions – from self-driving cars to mobile payments – have originated in San Francisco in recent years, it should only be a matter of time until fractional equity owner-ship spreads from California to the world. Shall we bet?

ASK BUDDIES, NOT BANKS: PEER-TO-PEER LENDING

Freelancers and people with volatile incomes may have a hard time getting a traditional mortgage. Banks typically ask for a long list of guarantees, such as regular paychecks, before they hand out money.

The sharing economy now offers an alternative: don't ask the bank, ask a crowd of people like you and me. The market for such "P2P lending" has been growing fast in recent years and it makes lending somewhat of a personal affair between buddies.

There is no middleman, only a person who needs money and a group of peers willing to pitch in. They meet each other on platforms such as Lending Club, Lending Crowd or Peer Street. It takes just a few clicks and often less than 24 hours to find enough private lenders. Some people finance their mortgage deposit this way, while others secure business loans as large as half a million dollars.

Of course, borrowing from peers also has a price. The lenders typically need to see some sort of security – a motorcycle or a car. And just as with a traditional method, borrowers need to pay back the loan plus interest. However, many get more leeway and pay less than the stock-standard bank rate. That's because P2P platforms run their own checks on the creditworthiness of a borrower and assign interest rates based on personal circumstances.

Peer lenders tend to accept people with lower credit scores who'd only find closed doors in a traditional bank. That said, be prepared to pay more if your credit score is lousy. At SocietyOne, an Australian P2P lender, peers currently charge almost 20 per cent interest for the riskiest 5-year loans.[19]

A new high-tech shadow market for lending? Financial watchdogs have been eyeing the industry closely, since it's still in its infancy and not yet properly covered by existing regulations. While P2P loan portfolios are very different from the toxic debts that caused the Global Financial Crisis, regulators remain concerned about any type of high-risk lending.

Regulatory issues aside, the new kids on the lending block show that things are moving forward. Fintechs are increasingly attuned to the needs of the Flow Generation with its growing number of freelancers and contractors who may be struggling to secure traditional mortgages. Of course, P2P loans have also become appealing to property investors, who realise that helping a stranger scramble together the mortgage for his house might be much more profitable than buying a house themselves.

CROWD HELP ME

P2P loans, like traditional mortgages, need to be paid back dollar by dollar. Pure crowdfunding models, on the other hand, let borrowers set the repayment terms.

What started as a fringe financing concept for dreamers with wacky ideas but no money has grown into a valid fundraising concept that can mobilise masses on a global stage. Campaigns presented with charm and compelling arguments can be surprisingly successful. You can decide to brew your own gin in an old garage, seek cash for the first batch of booze, and find a willing crowd of takers on platforms like Kickstarter or Indiegogo. Or you could sail around the world for charity and promise your crowd investors nothing but a postcard in return.

In 2017, a children's book about "rebel girls", featuring tales of famous women like Queen Elizabeth and Beyoncé, became the fastest-funded published project in Kickstarter history at the time, topping $100,000 in just a few hours and nearly $900,000 in total. Anyone who chipped in $25 received a hardcover copy in return.[20]

Every year, several such campaigns manage to raise over a million dollars each.

No surprise that cash-strapped home buyers are joining the scene, hoping to finance their mortgages with the help of a crowd that accepts looser repayment rules than traditional lenders. They still have a hard time on mainstream crowdfunding platforms, though. Who has the spare cash to finance a stranger's dream home? Many people prefer to fund social entrepreneurs with a selfless cause.

***

That's what Australian Gold Coast girl Caitlin Argyle learned. A few years ago, when she was just 17 and crowdfunding still a novelty, Caitlin attempted her own campaign on Indiegogo, causing a nationwide press frenzy.[21]

TV teams and newspaper reporter featured her plea for strangers to chip in toward a A$48,000 deposit, which would let her buy a A$400,000 house in a subtropical part of Australia famous for surf, sandy beaches, and vibrant nightlife.

The Gold Coast is a tourist magnet, and Caitlin tried to make it work in her favour. In exchange for donations, she offered holiday accommodations in her future home. As an extra incentive, for every 10 weeks of holidays booked, she promised to give a family in need a free stay for a week. She also offered to give funders "virtual hugs", iron their shirts and entertain their kids at birthday parties.

"I am so excited!" Caitlin announced on her fundraising page when she launched it. "If I wait until I save the money up from working, it will take me many years to raise a deposit."

But the campaign never took off. After a couple of months Caitlin shut it down. She had raised just 6,125 Australian dollars.

***

The market has evolved since Caitlin first tried her luck. In recent years, specialist real estate crowdfunding sites have emerged around the globe, such as PropertyPartner in the United Kingdom and Housers in Spain. Most of them target professional investors who want to buy into real estate developments. However, some startups are now helping ordinary people crowdfund their mortgage.

On HomeFundIt, a subsidiary of Californian group CMG Financial, ordinary Americans can hit their social networks with a heartfelt story and raise funds for the down payment on a property of their choice – as a donation, without having to pay it back.

HomeFundIt even offers coaching on how to craft a convincing campaign strategy that resonates with a target audience. One buyer, for example, realised that his fellow churchgoers were more inclined to donate after he handed them flyers with a weblink to his campaign website. Hundreds of families successfully secured a mortgage with crowdfunding appeals, says the firm.

Asking friends and family for help may be awkward. But why not? When something really matters, when we have a dream and know we cannot achieve it alone, many of us do it. Those are the moments when we have the guts to write that one uncomfortable email or pick up the phone. And we may realise in the end that our social networks make us richer than we think.

HOME SWEET HOSTEL

In the sharing economy nothing goes to waste. Unloved

clothes, empty car seats, vacant rooms – digital platforms help us turn all sorts of underused assets into money.

The sharing business has now become so profitable it's caught the eye of the home loan industry. Aware that many aspiring property buyers are struggling to secure a traditional mortgage, a Seattle-based startup called Loftium is proposing a deal: we help you with your down payment if you, in turn, rent out a spare bedroom in your new house and split the proceeds with us.

Loftium gives real estate buyers a cash injection of up to $50,000 for the down payment on a house, as long as they commit to listing an extra room on Airbnb for up to three years. In the best case, the rental business generates enough income to repay Loftium's loan. If it doesn't, despite everyone's best efforts, the firm bears the risk.

In a nod to the growing gig and sharing economy, traditional mortgage lenders, including US-based Quicken Loans and Citizens Bank, have begun to partner with Airbnb.[22] These firms offer lower mortgage rates to people who regularly generate income with Airbnb rentals. Even America's government-backed mortgage lender Fannie Mae recently started a pilot program, in which Airbnb hosts can now qualify for better mortgage deals.[23]

While these programs target existing homeowners – people who already have a mortgage and a house – they hint at a bigger shift in the lending industry worldwide. Startups and century-old institutions alike are adapting to the reality of shared bedrooms and Netflix accounts in creative ways. They have to, because the gig economy keeps growing. Over two-thirds (71%) of American lenders said that in 2018 they have had borrowers apply for a mortgage with income from the gig economy, according to Fannie Mae.[24]

Subletting rooms may not appeal to everyone. Some people are keen to design their home as a private sanctuary, one exclusively theirs. However, for the Flow Generation exclusive ownership is losing its lustre anyway, and we are now looking at different questions. How badly do we want to own a house? And how much personal privacy are we willing to sacrifice, even if only for a while?

Join a modern housing community

The musicians arrive with amplifiers and egg shakers. They take their guitars out of the bulky cases and plug in their microphones in the shed, between the canisters of resin and spray paint that the boys use for surfboard repairs.

By nightfall, the garden will have turned into a stage. There will be Brazilian singers and beatboxers, a hundred smiling faces and broken glass. Hosting charity concerts has become the social fabric of the share house.

Vera closes her eyes. Just a few years ago she was still carrying the baby in a sling around her body, navigating a moonlit backyard full of people cheering and helloing each other over the clank of ice cubes in their drinks. She chases away thoughts of the messy clean-up awaiting her the next day.

It's part of the deal. Even the comments from outsiders who doubt this living model: "A share house with kids? Sounds pretty tribal."

It's what you get when you choose to share your family home. You share more than the space. More than the rent. You take your idea of life and merge it with others'. You share heartbreaks and job worries and gastro bugs. And before you know it, your housemates are family.

Some days her long-term housemate Max would take the kids slacklining in the park or jumping on the abandoned mattress on the clifftops overlooking the ocean. Don't they say it takes a village to raise a child? The Brazilian singer warms up her voice. Where are the children? Vera's eyes wander. Then she spots them, in between the other musicians, egg shakers in their hands and pride in their faces at being part of the band.

***

Shared living, once the exclusive domain of hippies and students, has become a normality for many urban creatives and location-independent professionals. They marry financial necessity with a deep-seated desire for social connection.

Urban planners and property developers think this lifestyle is set to become more common in the future.

Even the world's largest furniture retailer, Ikea, is bracing for a world where living space is shrinking and we may need to give up entire rooms as we snuggle closer to our neighbours. "In the future you may not need a kitchen because you can go to a communal area to cook or heat up your ready-made meal", predicts Tiffany Buckins, head of interior design at Ikea Australia.[25]

Why pay full real estate dollars or rental rates if we can get cheaper housing that, on top of it, gives our lives a social boost? Who cares if we have to go back to sharing frying pans or fridges or toilets as people did back in the days when scarcity was the norm?

Up until a few decades ago, some East Berliners had to go to public swimming pools for a shower because their flats had none. That was life after the war, in a bombed-out city, under a communist regime. Today, we live in abundance. Yet urbanisation and erratic income streams are challenging our living conditions and shared amenities are returning as a way of modern life.

Property developers and startups are responding. They convert old buildings or barren acreage into hip communal living spaces. Co-living means sharing the same roof with others. Co-housing, in contrast, means living in separate homes with shared community services and spaces. Both are back in vogue.

Let's have a look at the details.

CO-LIVING

Nicoló realised the washing machine was missing only one week after he had moved to New York. He looked for it in the kitchen. Then in the bathroom. Then in the corridor. It was nowhere to be found. He stared helplessly at the only closed door in the apartment, the one leading into the bedroom of his flatmate Paul, a taxi driver in his 40s with a passion for Chinese takeaway food. Paul found him right there, holding a bunch of dirty clothes.

"What are you doing?" Paul asked.

"Ahem, looking for the washing machine?"

"It ain't here, Prince Charming. You gotta go to the laundromat down the street."

Nicoló gave him a puzzled look. He was used to living in share houses without a washing machine when he was a student in Milan, but he didn't expect that grown-up professionals in New York's Greenwich Village, where rent was the highest he had ever paid, would still be living the laundromat life.

Paul must have read his mind.

"Everybody does it," he said. "We don't have space for this bulky stuff, not even in the building. Space is expensive. Welcome to Manhattan".

***

Shared homes and services are not special to Manhattan. They appeal in every neighbourhood where desirability, urban density and strict zoning laws combine to make prices unaffordable.

There, property developers and other firms are now fueling the co-living trend. They create custom-built shared accommodations for people who seek convenience, kumbaya or both. Worldwide, the six biggest co-living companies alone plan to house more than a quarter million residents in 2019.[26]

In Barcelona, managers at co-living space A Landing Pad have converted a white city house into a breezy temporary home for digital nomads. Bedrooms with ensuite (and funky wall art) cost 500 to 1,100 euros per month. On the sunny terrace, guests can work on wooden furniture or chill in a hammock. Don't confuse A Landing Pad with a backpacker hostel. This is a purpose-built venue for The Flow Generation's laptop workers: highly autonomous people who are travelling far and wide, and yet long for a community of kindred spirits. Minimum stay is one month.[27]

Lonely nomads will find their flock in Casa Netural, a four-storey co-living/co-working house in Matera, a southern Italian city whose heritage and beauty just earned it the title "European Capital of Culture". If you stay here, you get your own bedroom for 500 euros a month. You share living, cooking, bathrooms and working areas. The website is full of videos of pasta nights held in the common kitchen.

Co-living makes housing more affordable – and sociable. It can even be a bridge between young and old. The Dutch city of Deventer, for example, offers free accommodation in a local nursing home to students who agree to spend 30 hours each month with senior residents. Some watch soccer games on TV or cook with the elderly, others teach them computer skills or simply laze on a bench under the trees.

For Gea Sijpkes, the nursing home's director, the model is a cure against loneliness, and a win-win across generations. "The students bring the outside world in. There is lots of warmth in the contact," she told local reporters.[28]

CO-HOUSING: VILLAGE, NOT VILLA

"What's it like to live here?" Vera asked the twin boys. They had appeared on their bikes in a cloud of dust, from somewhere further down the dry grassland, barefoot and bare-chested, their long blond hair flying behind them in the wind. One carried a bowl of popcorn in a crate on his bike, the other a microscope.

The boys know every corner and every cow grid on this vast acreage far from the next big city. They came here five years ago with their parents, joining a communal living and land sharing co-operative that offers an alternative to the crowded and overpriced housing in Australia's metropoles.

Its residents are as diverse as the houses they have built on this vast rural land, off the grid, sustained by solar power and rainwater. There are freelancers and families, retirees and tradespeople, free-spirited travellers and university scientists. Some houses are quirky, made out of clay and straw, framed by banana plants and lemon trees. Others are sleek and modern, with large wooden decks that can compete with Sydney's expensive waterfront bungalows.

You have to apply to join the community and show that you're willing to pitch in. On Saturdays, residents get together to weed the playground, clear overgrown fire trails and maintain community buildings.

Sounds hippie? "It's really nice," said one of the twins, as he picked up his bike and his popcorn, and Vera watched them ride away towards the dam where the kangaroos had found some green shoots.

***

Housing co-operatives like this one sell land at a fraction of the price city dwellers pay for a block. They prove that it's still possible to own a dream house – if we think beyond the property market we are familiar with.

There are co-housing communities for every taste and budget. Commercial property developers build some of them and offer houses that cost just as much as those in regular residential neighbourhoods. But many are run as not-for-profit collectives that aim to make housing more affordable and sustainable.

For example, La Borda is a young housing cooperative featuring 28 newly built apartments in a working-class neighbourhood of Barcelona.

The development sets a countertrend to property speculation and rising rents. Instead, it promotes a novel way of living together: as part of a non-profit community with a social bond. The land belongs to the municipality, which leases out apartments for 75 years. Social entrepreneurs, ethical banks and private donors have helped fund the project. [29]

"We want to show that we can succeed without following the path dictated by the market or traditional practices," said the project's architect, Carles Baiges Camprubí.[30]

Co-housing is spreading fast around the world. In the UK, a report by insurance firm Towergate counts as many as 60 new co-housing developments currently planned or under construction, on top of more than a dozen existing ones. In the Netherlands, co-housing projects are expected to more than double from 30 to 70 in coming years. The American market is burgeoning too. Here, co-housing communities are set to grow to more than 230, from 100 today, according to the report.

The force behind this trend? It's not just about cheaper rent. It's also about rekindling human connections. "Cohousing is a way of resolving the isolation many people experience today, recreating the neighbourly support of the past," says the British Co-Housing Network.[31]

Space10, a think tank set up by Ikea to research how people will live in cities in the future, has no doubt that the co-housing trend is here to stay. "The rise of the sharing economy suggests that people are ready to share more than we thought," the firm says in a report.

The Danish capital Copenhagen is often seen as the cradle of co-housing. For decades, its colourful district Freetown Christiania formed a bulwark against capitalism and individualistic consumption.

Founded in 1971 as an anarchic commune on deserted military land, Christiania's residents dreamt of creating a different society from scratch. They rejected property rights and car traffic. Instead, they embraced self-sufficient living and a spirit of looking after each other. Those who had joined Christiania lived in their own houses, but shared common spaces such as saunas, workshops and playgrounds. They also shared cleaning duties, took turns babysitting or tended vegetable gardens together. The community even organised its own social services, including recycling and waste collection.

Those days now belong to the past. Christiania's residents eventually bowed to government pressure to buy the land they had been squatting on. Many houses are now fenced. Tourists roam the public spaces and police patrols increased after open cannabis use in the neighbourhood escalated into a full-blown drug trade.

Still, the concept of shared property is very much alive in Denmark. More than 700 co-housing communities exist in the Nordic country and the number is growing.[32] Eight out of 100 Danes are currently living in a co-housing development of some sort.[33] And many of them will tell you that their way of life, though rooted in a socialist utopia, is first and foremost one thing: pragmatic.

***

Ask Claus Borup Skovsgaard, a 47-year old physiotherapist, who lives with his wife and three children in a slim, two-storey house in Lange Eng, one of the country's young and modern co-housing communities a short tram ride from Copenhagen. His little villa, clad in dark timber, with lots of glass and steel, looks like his neighbour's. And the one next to it. And the one opposite. Built wall to wall, the units form a ring around a shared wildflower garden, creating a gigantic play area for the many kids growing up in Lange Eng. There are no fences and no curtains, just one big open space girded by those who live here.

The openness scared them at first. The idea of living close up with 200 strangers looking into each other's garden and living rooms. "Would we get along with them? My wife was very apprehensive," says Claus. They found Lange Eng by chance seven years ago, on a drive into the countryside in search of a place to start a family away from city traffic and sickening mortgage costs.

Today, the Skovsgaards couldn't imagine settling anywhere else. They praise the openness they so dreaded at the start. Several nights a week, they join the open dinner in the communal kitchen next to the communal cinema and gym. Every fifth week it's their turn to cook. Other than that, they now skip much of the shopping and preparing meals. It's all taken care of, so they have more time to cuddle their children or catch up with neighbours. Most are young families and many are digital workers, getting jobs done on a laptop from home. Claus's wife, a teacher, is studying for a master's degree after work.

Houses in Lange Eng cost less than in Copenhagen, but more than those in the immediate neighbourhood. Still, the model has become a drawcard. Claus says you can't beat the benefits of co-housing for people with busy lives: "Open space gives an open mind. It's very healthy to live in this kind of environment." The last time Claus looked it up, 400 names were on the community's waiting list.

***

Years after Inbal, the Israeli girl, left her family's kibbutz, communal living is making a comeback across the Western world. Will she, one day perhaps, return with her children to the community she grew up in? What would Heraclitus, Nietzsche, Vico and the Goddess of Never-Not-Broken make of our times? Is there a red

248

thread connecting all these legends and myths, the philosophers and the life stories of people like us?

It's hard to put an end to a river that is constantly flowing. It's impossible to forecast the definitive shape of a liquid life. We can only take a picture of it, right now, in this moment. And even that may be blurry, like an impressionistic painting that gives us only a notion of movement, light, and direction.

Many people are scared of the future, but many others anticipate it with eager smiles and eyes wide open. They enjoy the opportunities technology brings. Yet they also revel in the sense of belonging to a new generation of self-aware and sociable people, who are finding their flow with the help of like-minded others. They band together for a project or for life, supporting each other in their endeavours as the waters around them keep shifting.

If you don't become the ocean,
you will get seasick every day.
−Leonard Cohen

Stories from the Flow Generation

Going with the flow

There's only one way forward in dealing with turbulent times: we need to give up resistance and become ourselves fluid like water.

We are eternally in flow. Let's go with it. We are the Flow Generation.

ADRIÁN. MADRID. MAKING A WISH.

It's gotten cold in the capital and dark. The frenzied shouting of the hawkers selling tickets for the Christmas lottery has died down, but the chestnut vendors are still there. They are firing up their wheeled tin ovens, infusing the afternoon fog with a sweet, wooden taste.

A few days before the university spilled out all staff and students for the winter break, one of the senior professors stopped Adrián on the floor.

"There's never been an associate professor who worked so much for such little money," he told him. He wanted to make Adrián feel good, show him how much he appreciated his dedication. But neither he nor Adrián have a say over the future of his teaching role. It may evaporate as fast as it came and remain just that: one more opportunity to learn something new and try out new skills.

Adrián feels more optimistic than a year ago. Not safe. But stronger. So, when the bell on the clock tower on Madrid's town hall strikes midnight, he makes a wish: "I hope that soon there will be a new door, one that is stable and does not have loose hinges." Then he eats 12 grapes for good luck, as every good Spaniard does on New Year's Eve, to mark the passage of time.

ALESSANDRO. AMSTERDAM. UNBOXED.

They say it takes just seven seconds for people to form an opinion about you. Seven seconds to make an impression. How do you want to be seen? Do you dare to reveal all your broken pieces?

Up on stage, invited as guest speaker by a big law firm, Alessandro refuses to make sense. The auditorium is packed with corporate lawyers. They came to learn about popular blockchain myths and Alessandro, they were told, would bust them all.

Who is this guy? He is wearing a dark suit and crisp white shirt. But his wrist exposes a big waterproof surf watch and his hair is tousled. One of his clients introduces him as "our house lawyer: sometimes he's there, sometimes he is not there". The client praises his flexibility. Alessandro smiles.

Recently he resolved some urgent legal issues from his iPad while jolting in a four-wheel drive across the Namibian desert on the hunt for some strong Atlantic wind. He defies expectations and the more he works without a fixed schedule or location, the more he gets people talking.

In the networking break lawyers swarm around him, asking more questions about his career than his speech. "So... you are an in-house legal consultant working externally for various companies?" It's become a pattern and it amuses Alessandro that many professionals get lost when they cannot put him in a box. He has noticed people want crisp definitions about themselves and others to feel comfortable.

And he?

Somewhere between Brisbane, Cape Town and Amsterdam, Alessandro simply stopped defining what exactly it is he does.

He is as much a lawyer as a solopreneur, a startup consultant, tech advisor, traveller, kite-surf instructor, eternal student and free spirit. He just does what he enjoys and it energises him to think that, three years after leaving the corporate world, he is finally making a decent living on his own.

"Being anything you want is a scary thought for the ones seeking the illusion of certainty," says Alessandro. "Because when there is no certainty you can't really make plans. You must be willing to let go of control and trust."

LACHLAN. GLASGOW. EDINBURGH. IN BETWEEN.

He has almost reached the end of train and by now he's ready to travel standing. If he leans back against the rattling wall, feet firmly planted on the grimy carriage floor, he can manage to balance his laptop on his knees.

The hydraulic door opens with a hiss. And when it shuts again, cold Scottish air sucking at his cheeks, Lachlan finally spots a seat. He slumps down and checks his phone.

Less than an hour now to Edinburgh.

Going with the flow

Not even a year has passed since he left Singapore. He wanted more freedom to try himself out. See if he could grow beyond himself and start his own online media and marketing firm. He knew he had the skills, the ambition, the entrepreneurial streak, and some money saved. What he didn't have was the right visa.

Lachlan moved back to Europe. But this morning he wonders if he has ever arrived. He spends most of his week on railways, zipping between his parents' house in Glasgow and his girlfriend's place in Edinburgh. He works in transit and from old colonial buildings that his bank has converted into coworking lounges free of charge. A few times each month, he rides further along the rugged coast to meet his business partner in Aberdeen.

His lives a life in between. He had the courage to start from scratch – once again. Now he's rolling, but he hasn't reached his destination yet. There's not one place he can call home.

During the harsh Scottish winter, when grey clouds hung over the frozen cow pastures like lead, Lachlan silently cursed the lack of stability in his life. Who doesn't? "Everybody hates uncertainty. As human beings, we are creatures of comfort," he says.

Before he can finish the sentence, his phone rings. His business partner is on the line. "Let's hire the guy in China," he prompts, excitement in his voice. Their team of virtual assistants and content creators is growing. They have momentum. And when he hangs up, close to Edinburgh main station, Lachlan looks reassured, ready to tackle any obstacle that may come his way.

"Big things are built one brick at a time," he says, grabs his laptop bag and lets the passenger stream carry him out of the train and onto the solid platform.

VERA. SYDNEY. FINDING LAND.

The first thing they noticed was the tree. Ten men tall, with gnarly branches and smooth skin, it had conquered the entire block. FOR SALE said the sign near its trunk. And then, a few weeks later, when they had really done it – transferred the money, signed the papers and endured the real estate agent's incessant smile – a sticker overwrote the message: SOLD.

It was a fuzzy idea at first, hatched by a group of architect friends getting drunk in a hot tub in the rainforest garden of a holiday house. "Why don't we buy land here and build something ourselves?"

They talked all night, hot-headedly, infected by the thought. Here, hours away from the next big city, you could still snatch up a vacant lot for sums that would barely make a mortgage deposit in Sydney. Vera and her partner Lars grabbed the opportunity. Year after year of living in the share house they had put money aside. A safety cushion for when the landlord might cancel the lease. Enough to buy "that small piece of dirt", they joked. But they were serious.

Every weekend they drove up the coast to build a place they could call their own. They felled the tree and bought a trampoline to keep the kids busy, while the adults were painting and drilling, plastering walls and laying floorboards. Friends helped heave beams into place and wheelbarrow soil around. When the house was done, it wasn't just theirs. It was a community effort.

"And now?" asked Vera. "Shall we build another share house?" They sat on the wooden deck and watched the bats emerge from the rainforest canopy. Black silhouettes flying into the twilight. The sky, a wide-open canvas. "We can do anything," replied Lars. "Anything we want."

Conclusion

When the idea for this book was born, on a wild beach on Australia's South Coast, we had a different title in mind: *Precariously Ever After?*

For us, it was the key question that guided us through writing this book and in Italian it sounds even more provocative: *Precari e contenti?*. Precarious and happy – is it possible to be both? Can you really feel at ease when life as you know it is falling apart and the only thing you hear from experts is that the future will be shaky terrain?

Just like many of the people we interviewed, we started at a point of confusion and fear. We realised we would never be able to live like our parents, who spent decades in the same job and enjoyed much certainty about their life paths. Our generation, in contrast, appears lost. New technology and increasingly unpredictable economies have swept away the sense that there is a safe and clear path to retirement. And even if there were, many of us wouldn't want it anymore.

We've grown up in an age of change. Yet, like many of our protagonists, we're still learning to get used to it. Even embrace it. Both of us quit our full-time jobs to focus on this book. We wanted to give it our best shot. And, frankly, we also wanted to prove to ourselves that we could jump into the darkness and still find our feet. That we could get comfortable with ambiguity, and trust our skills and our passions above anything else.

In the last few months, we ourselves have experimented with alternative and precarious ways of making a living outside the corporate frame: as digital nomads and freelancers. We have given surf lessons and semi-nars on storytelling. None of these gigs will last forever, but they were (and are) a lot of fun and have taught us some valuable lessons. We've written this book from our laptops, meeting halfway around the globe: in tropical Bali, in Southern Italy and in the Australian wilderness.

Ultimately, though, this book has written us more than we have written it. And we both feel very grateful for what yoga teachers and energy healers would call "journey of self-discovery".

This book has taught us how to go with the flow of life. This doesn't mean we're surrendering to fate. "Going with the flow" in our book means accepting that there are some things we cannot change or foresee. It means finding an inner strength amid the outer turmoil and seeing life as a constant opportunity for learning and reinvention. It's about resilience, not resistance. It's about replacing fear and confusion with optimism and trust.

We hope this book inspires readers as much as it has inspired us. It wouldn't exist without the support of many people who believed in this project as much as we did. We want to thank you. For the help and the hugs. For your contacts and critical opinions. For your encouragement and expertise. And for reminding us, in moments of doubt and in the spirit of this book, that everything you dream of is possible.

Nicoló and Vera

Afterword

By Stefano Scarpetta, Director for Employment, Labour and Social Affairs at the OECD

The world of work is in flux. For all the signs that labour markets are improving in many OECD countries, digital technology is profoundly changing our economies. The diversity of employment contracts is greater than ever. Remote working technology and the emergence of the platform economy offer unparalleled opportunities for both workers and employers. However, there is also the risk that a highly digitalised, automated and ultra-flexible labour market could leave behind some workers or see their rights and protections undermined.

What will the future bring?

There is a lot of uncertainty about the speed and depth of the digital transformation, and even more on the impact it will have on jobs. Let me point out two controversial trends.

First, at the aggregate level, our data has not yet pointed to a risk of massive technological unemployment (as John Maynard Keynes foresaw in an essay in 1931). Quite to the contrary, OECD countries are on average experiencing record-high employment rates.

And yet a look beyond the aggregate employment data shows that for a growing number of young people the access to the traditional labour market is blocked. For many youths – especially the low-skilled or those living in disadvantaged areas – it is getting harder to find permanent full-time work. They often get stuck on a parallel track of the job market, where they only find temporary, casual and contract jobs. This is an acute problem in Southern Europe, but also in Japan.

Secondly, there is the hype about the platform and gig economy. Certainly, there is an increase in a certain type of new, flexible employment, but it is difficult to pinpoint the true size of platform work. Our best estimates show that the platform economy, while growing fast, only makes up a tiny fraction of the labour market. And since we don't see a sharp decline in aggregate full-time employment, we have no clear evidence to suggest that the gig economy is expanding at the expense of the traditional standard job.

What we do observe is a significant increase in very short-term contracts with a duration of just one month. These high-frequency, very short-term jobs are extremely precarious.

The data is ambiguous and this also has to do with the design of official labour market surveys. There are now so many new forms of employment and such a large number of different job models that survey respondents simply don't know what to answer. Some people state they work full-time, based on the hours they work. Yet in reality many hold a part-time job and supplement their income with platform work. We have to assume that some official surveys distort the reality.

Still, the world of work is changing and we have to adapt. We need a Copernican Revolution in which workers put themselves at the centre and engage in life-long learning (with adequate support for those who cannot support themselves). We will all be in charge of developing our own human capital more than in the past. The problem is that employees are not used to being in charge. They are used to having an employer who tells them what they need. This is a challenge.

We also need new tools to navigate the uncertainty. Platforms, companies and governments need to ensure that there is more protection and support for the self-employed. Traditional social programs have been designed to protect traditional workers in a stable employee-employer relationship – not the modern independent worker.

Several countries have in recent years introduced new unemployment insurance systems based on individual savings accounts for each worker. In Chile, employers are obliged to pay the insurance contributions for workers on atypical contracts. France just expanded its model of personalised training accounts to include self-employed workers. Singapore offers every citizen a lifelong learning credit.

There is a solution. The digital economy may make it easier for people to acquire new skills. In the future, we will think less in terms of professions and more in terms of skills and competences. When we do this and focus on the actual tasks people do in their jobs, we find that many professions require very similar skill sets. Take me, for example. I'm an economist, but the skills I need in my current role would also serve me in a different context.

What's missing still are more data analytics tools to help workers assess which of their skills are relevant for which job. This would be hugely useful for people who have to develop their own work and study path. To be sure, official tools are not yet widely available. But they don't have to be. Workers can easily do a skills assessment themselves.

The technology is there. The data are there. The opportunities to succeed in the changing world of work are there.

Acknowledgements

W e would like to give special thanks to our editor, Dan McNeill, for his wit and wordcraft and for his boundless motivation. James Crabtree for his extraordinary help in sharpening our thoughts and for getting our proposal into shape. Stefano Solarino for a beautifully flowing cover design. Lachlan Lewis Hay for his marketing expertise. Simon Docherty for believing in us and muscling in on the publishing industry. Andrew Charlton and Fraser Thompson for paving the ground for us to meet and for inspiring us to find new answers to the big economic questions of our times. Ajithkumar Dhevarajan, Abhinav Singh Bhal, Maria Cabral, Bintang Mulyasakti for early social media support. Laura Ruiz for her spirit and for reminding us of our bond. Marco J. Aboav for guiding us through the alternative investment jungle. Cameron Barrie for sharing his spark of knowledge in the algorithmic hotdog-not-hotdog world. Upasana Mukherjee for background research on P2P insurances. Astitva Tyagi, Kevin Burns and Jayant Ramanand, also known as "the CUHK book worms", for voracious curiosity and precious research help. Martina Lovascio for accepting the massive challenge of translating the entire manuscript into Italian. Elisabeth Claire Goost for her enthusiasm in tackling the German translation. Nicolò Muciaccia for all those runs and chats by the sea, and for helping us understand legal issues related to the data deluge. Josefin Nordlander for bringing magic and her first aid kit to this journey. Gemma Hogan for enlightening excursions into Hindu mythology. Lars Goldstein for his unconditional love, in high tide and in low tide, and for lending his sharp eye for design to improve this book's layout. Francesca Addante for the love and serenity she poured into Nicoló's life. Our dads for the constant and precious intellectual challenges, and our mums for believing in this project, sometimes even more than ourselves. And all the protagonists in this book who agreed to share their life stories.

Endnotes

Turbulent Times

1 Nathan Bennett and G. James Lemoine (2014), 'What VUCA Really Means for You', *Harvard Business Review*, January/February.

2 WEF (2018), 'World Enters Critical Period of Intensified Risks in 2018', press release, 17 January.

3 Angel Gurría (2018), *New Year's Wishes*, speech, 30 January.

4 Christopher Ingraham (2017), 'This is what Americans are afraid of in the age of Trump', *Washington Post*, 20 October.

5 Brice Stokes, Richard Wike and Jacob Poushter (2016), 'Europeans see ISIS, climate change as most serious threats', *Pew Research Center*, 13 June.

6 McKinsey Global Institute (2015), The new global competition for corporate profits.

7 See, for example, Justin Fox (2017), 'The Fall, Rise and Fall of Creative Destruction', *Bloomberg*, 26 September.

8 Julie L. Hotchkiss and Christopher J. Macpherson (2015), 'Falling Job Tenure: Labor as Just another Commodity', *Federal Reserve Bank of Atlanta*, blog, 8 June.

9 Eurofound (2015), *Job tenure in turbulent times*, Publications Office of the European Union.

10 David Harrison and Eric Morath (2018), 'In This Economy, Quitters Are Winning', *The Wall Street Journal*, 4 July.

11 McCridle (2014), *Job mobility in Australia*, blog, 18 June.

12 Benjamin Mullin (2016), 'The Washington Post is using robots to cover the Olympics and the election', *Poynter*, 5 August.

13 Stefan Hall (2018), 'AI will write a best-seller by 2049, experts predict', *World Economic Forum*, 1 March.

14 Thomas Friedman (2015), 'Moore's Law turns 50', *The New York Times*, 13 May.

15 Edward Lorenz (1972), *American Association for the Advancement of Science*, meeting note, 29 December, http://eaps4.mit.edu/research/Lorenz/Butterfly_1972.pdf

16 Interactive Schools (2018), '50 million users: how long does it take tech to reach this milestone?', blog, 8 February.

17 Zeynep Tufekci and Christopher Wilson (2012), 'Social media and the decision to participate in political protest: observations from Tahrir Square', *Journal of Communication*, 6 March.

18 Michel Syrett and Marion Devine/The Economist (2012), *Managing Uncertainty*.

19 Media Education Foundation (2010), interview with George Gerbner, see transcript: www.mediaed.org/transcripts/Mean-World-Syndrome-Transcript.pdf.

20 World Bank (2019), *World Development Report 2019. The Changing Nature of Work*, p. 22.

21 OECD (2016), Back to work: Denmark. Improving the Re-employment Prospects of Displaced Workers, 'Foreword'.

22 World Bank (2019): *World Development Report 2019*, p.17.

23 Daniel Tencer (2017), '85% of jobs that will exist in 2030 haven't been invented yet: Dell', *Huffington Post*, 14 July. See also: Institute for The Future/Dell Technologies (2017), *Emerging Technologies Impact on Society and Work in 2030*.

24 James Pethokoukis (2016), 'What the story of ATMs and bank tellers reveals about the 'rise of the robots' and jobs', *American Enterprise Institute*, 6 June.

25 Janet Fairweather (1973), *The Death of Heraclitus*, http://grbs.library.duke.edu/article/viewFile/9121/4593.

26 McKinsey Global Institute (2015), The new global competition for corporate profits.

27 Tom Goodwin (2015), 'The battle is for the customer interface', *Techcrunch*, 3 March.

28 Stephen Hall, Dan Lovallo, and Reinier Musters (2012), 'How to put your money where your strategy is' *McKinsey Quarterly.*

Jagged Career

1 Eurostat (2018), 'Share of young adults aged 18-34 living with their parents by age and sex', EU-SILC Survey, http://ec.europa.eu/eurostat/web/products-datasets/-/ilc_lvps08 [last update: 5 June 2019].

2 Statistics Canada (2017), 'Young adults living with their parents in Canada in 2016', *Census in brief*, 2 August.

3 Upwork/Freelancers Union (2017), *Freelancing in America 2017.*

4 The share of permanent full-time work in the EU declined to 59% in 2014, from 62% in 2003. See: European Parliament (2016), *Precarious Employment in Europe*, p. 58.

5 Ibid.

6 OECD (2018), *The Future of Social Protection: What works for non-standard workers?*, policy brief on the future of work.

7 Institut für Arbeitsmarkt- und Berufsforschung (2018), 'Befristungen erreichten 2017 einen neuen Höchststand', press release, 3 July.

8 Australia Institute (2018), 'For first time, less than half of workers have a standard job', press release, 29 May.

9 European Parliament (2016), *Precarious Employment in Europe*, p.59.

10 Preston Lauterbach (2011), *The Chitlin' Circuit: And the Road to Rock 'n' Roll.* New York: W.W. Norton.

11 European Parliament (2016), *Precarious Employment in Europe*, p. 20.

12 Stanford, Jim (2018), 'Subsidising billionaires. Simulating the net incomes of UberX drivers', *Australia Institute.*

13 UK House of Commons. Work and Pensions Committee (2017), *Self-employment and the gig economy*, p. 14.
14 Ibid, p.8.
15 Deutscher Gewerkschaftsbund (2018), 'Wider die Tarifflucht – Tarifbindung stärken!', 6 April.
16 David Bell, David Blanchflower (2018), 'Underemployment in the US and Europe', *NBER Working Paper*, No. 24927.
17 Eurostat (2018), *EU labour market 2017. Underemployment and potential additional labour force*, https://ec.europa.eu/eurostat/statistics-explained/index.php/Underemployment_and_potential_additional_labour_force_statistics#Underemployed_part-time_workers [data extracted in May 2018].
18 Bell/Blanchflower (2018).
19 Eurostat (2017), *Being young in Europe today. Labour market – access and participation*, https://ec.europa.eu/eurostat/statistics-explained/index.php?title=Being_young_in_Europe_today_-_labour_market_-_access_and_participation [data extracted in December 2017].
20 Eurostat (2017), *Europe 2020 indicators – employment.* https://ec.europa.eu/eurostat/statistics-explained/index.php/Europe_2020_indicators_-_employment [data extracted in June 2018].
21 International Labour Office (2016), Non-standard employment around the world: Understanding challenges, shaping prospects, p. 58.
22 See for example: OECD (2008), *Impact of the economic crisis on employment and unemployment in OECD countries.*
23 Finkelstein, Harley (2018), 'From side hustle to life's work – evolving the gig economy'. *Forbes*, 8 May.
24 International Labour Office (2016), *Non-standard employment around the world*, p. 57.
25 The market is forecast to grow at a rate of 5.4% from 2016 to 2020, reaching almost $5 trillion, according to

The Business Research Company as quoted by Marketresearch.com (2017), https://blog.marketresearch.com/5-major-trends-that-are-transforming-the-professional-services-market.

26 Upwork (2017), 'What are continent workers, and are they right for your company?', 1 August, www.upwork.com/hiring/enterprise/whats-a-contingent-worker-and-are-they-right-for-your-company/.

27 Foundation for European Progressive Studies/UNI Europea/University of Hertfordshire (2017), *Work in the European gig economy*, p. 18.

28 Otto Kässi and Vili Lehdonvirta (2016), 'Online labour index: measuring the online gig economy for policy and research', *Oxford Internet Institute*, 3 November.

29 Ravin Jesuthasan (2017), 'You may not be a disruptor, but you might find opportunities in the gig economy', *Willis Towers Watson*, 24 July.

30 Deloitte (2018), *The workforce ecosystem: Managing beyond the enterprise. Global human capital trends 2018*, 28 March.

31 Willis Towers Watson (2018), *Global Future of Work Survey*.

32 McKinsey Global Institute (2016), *Independent work: choice, necessity, and the gig economy*.

33 Boston Consulting Group (2019), *The new freelancers – tapping talent in the gig economy*. "Contrary to widespread assumptions, most freelancers we surveyed said they do not choose gig work for lack of better options. Often they freelance in addition to other work or full-time employment. For many freelancers, gig platforms fulfil goals, preferences, and needs beyond compensation. Those benefits, they said, include greater autonomy and flexibility in their work and private lives and better choices of work projects."

34 Cheryl Carleton and Mary Kelly (2016), Alternative work arrangements and job satisfaction. *Villanova School of Business Department of Economics and Statistics Working Paper Series*, No. 32, December.

35 Upwork (2017), 'Freelancers predicted to become US workforce majority within a decade', press release, 17 October, www.upwork.com/press/2017/10/17/freelancing-in-america-2017/. More recent data show that the youngest generation entering the workforce, Gen Z, is even more likely to choose freelance work, www.upwork.com/press/2018/10/31/freelancing-in-america-2018/.

36 Deloitte (2018), *Deloitte 2018 Millennial Survey*, p. 17.

A night in the penthouse

1 World Economic Forum/PWC (2017), *Collaboration in Cities: From Sharing to 'Sharing Economy'*, p.8.

2 Brook Larmer (2017). 'China's Revealing Spin on the Sharing Economy', *The New York Times*, 20 November.

3 As quoted by Sharing Espana (2015), 'España, un país con potencial para la sharing economy', 25 March. See also: Nielsen (2015), *Is sharing the new buying*.

4 Kleiner Perkins (2018), *Internet Trends 2018*, slide 130. https://www.kleinerperkins.com/perspectives/internet-trends-report-2018/.

5 Felix Richter (2018), 'The Global Rise of Bike-Sharing', *Statista*, 10 April.

6 For example, research by social scientists Beate Volker and Henk Flap on neighbourhoods in the Netherlands shows that community-based childcare initiatives are more likely to occur when official daycare facilities aren't available. Psychologists at the University of Berkeley, California, found that prosocial behaviour is higher among people who have less resources. See: Paul Piff et al. (2010), 'Having less, giving more: The influence of social class on prosocial behavior', Journal of Personality and Social Psychology.

7 World Economic Forum/PWC (2017), Collaboration in Cities: From Sharing to 'Sharing Economy', p.6.

8 Bettelheim, Bruno (2001), *The Children of the Dream*, p.15.

9 Danielle Todd (2012), 'You Are What You Buy:

Postmodern Consumerism and the Construction of Self', *University of Hawai'i at Hilo HOHONU*, Vol. 10.

10 Naomi Klein (1999), *No Logo. Taking Aim at the Brand Bullies,* Toronto: Knopf Canada.

11 Charlotte McDonald (2015), "How many earths do we need?' BBC News, 16 June.

12 Esteban Ortiz-Ospina and Max Roser (2017), 'Happiness and Life Satisfaction', *Our World in Data,* https://ourworldindata.org/happiness-and-life-satisfaction

13 Curtis Sittenfeld (2000), 'No-Brands-Land', *Fast Company,* 31 August.

14 Francesco Sarracino and Małgorzata Mikucka (2017) Social Capital in Europe from 1990 to 2012: Trends and Convergence, *Social Indicators Research,* Vol. 131, Issue 1, March, pp. 407-437. See also references to academic studies in Learning Mind (2019), 'How Consumerism and Materialism of Modern Society Make Us Unhappy, Lonely and Unconfident', https://www.learning-mind.com/consumerism-and-materialism-unhappy/.

15 UK Government (2018), 'PM commits to government-wide drive to tackle loneliness', press release, 17 January.

16 Nietzsche, Friedrich Wilhelm (1974). *The Gay Science.* New York: Vintage Books.

17 Nielsen (2014), *Global Consumers Embrace The Sharing Economy*

18 See 'company history' in the newsroom of the Uber website: www.uber.com/en-AU/newsroom/history/.

19 ING (2015), 'European sharing economy to grow by a third in the next 12 months', press release, 1 July.

20 See Harth website: www.harth.space/the-harth-mission.

21 Author's calculations on PWC (2015), 'The Sharing Economy', *Consumer Intelligence Series,* https://www.pwc.fr/fr/assets/files/pdf/2015/05/pwc_et_ude_sharing_economy.pdf, 44% consumers are familiar with the sharing economy and 43% say that owning feels like a burden.

Data universe

1 McKinsey & Co. (2018), *Achieving business impact with data*, p. 2.
2 Fascinating internet live stats on www.internetlivestats.com/one-second/#google-band.
3 ICD (2018), Revenues for big data and business analytics solutions forecast to reach $260 billion in 2022, press release, 15 August.
4 Dan Hill (2015), 'The Secret to Airbnb's pricing algorithm', *IEEE Spectrum*, 20 August.
5 Kinetic Super (2018), *Contingent Job Index*, March.
6 Tim Monteverde posted an angry response to his Deliveroo experience on Youtube: www.youtube.com/watch?v=YEXseFoTpvg
7 Stanford Graduate School of Business (2015), 'Michal Kosinski: Computers Are Better Judges of Your Personality Than Friends', *Insights,* 23 January.
8 Manifesto for Agile Software Development (2001): http://agilemanifesto.org/.
9 SmartCap Technologies is a leading producer of such helmets. See: www.smartcaptech.com/life-smart-cap/
10 A promotional video by logistics company DHL shows the array of wearable devices in warehouses: www.youtube.com/watch?v=wUWw3Hqt1aQ.
11 Amazon, in a statement provided to us, said, "The speculation in the press about this patent is misguided. We do not track nor do we have the intention to track the location of our associates. We develop and implement innovative technologies in our operations to enable an incredible customer experience and to enhance the safety and ergonomics of our processes. Every day at companies around the world, employees use handheld scanners to check inventory and fulfil orders. This idea, if implemented in the future, would improve this process for our fulfilment associates. By moving equipment to associates' wrists, we could free up their hands from scanners and their eyes from computer screens."

12 One such provider of emotional tracking and analysis software is Cogito Corp: www.cogitocorp.com/.

13 See country-specific surveys by TSheets on tracking in the workplace (2017): www.tsheets.com/ca-en/gps-survey and www.tsheets.com/uk-en/gps-survey.

14 There is ongoing debate in Upwork's user forum about this time tracker function: https://community.upwork.com/t5/Freelancers/Time-Tracker-2-snapshot-in-10-minutes-and-it-will-charge-client/td-p/458326

15 Rackspace/Institute of Management Studies at Goldsmiths, University London (2014), The human cloud at work. A study into the impact of wearable technologies in the workplace.

16 Amazon, in a statement provided to us, gave the following explanation: "Echo woke up due to a word in background conversation sounding like 'Alexa'. Then, the subsequent conversation was heard as a 'send message' request. At which point, Alexa said out loud 'To whom?' At which point, the background conversation was interpreted as a name in the customer's contact list. Alexa then asked out loud, '[contact name], right?' Alexa then interpreted background conversation as 'right'. As unlikely as this string of events is, we are evaluating options to make this case even less likely."

17 Rachel Botsman: 'Big data meets Big Brother as China moves to rate its citizens', Wired, 21 October.

18 The Information Commissioner's Office, the British data watchdog, ruled in 2017 that the NHS had failed to comply with privacy laws when it shared the hospital data of around 1.6 million patients with Google Deep Mind, an artificial intelligence company.See official statement: https://ico.org.uk/about-the-ico/news-and-events/news-and-blogs/2017/07/royal-free-google-deepmind-trial-failed-to-comply-with-data-protection-law/. In 2014, an independent review found that the NHS had repeatedly shared hospital data of millions of patients

with pharma companies and insurers. See: Sir Nick Partridge (2014), *Review of data releases by the NHS Information Centre*, 17 June.

19 Official info on the European Union's General Data Protection Regulation (GDPR): https://ec.europa.eu/commission/priorities/justice-and-fundamental-rights/data-protection/2018-reform-eu-data-protection-rules_en.

20 Edelman (2018), *Trust Barometer 2018. Special report brands and social media*, pp. 15 and 4.

21 Focus (2018), 'Internet: Hälfte der Nutzer erwägt Social-Media-Abmeldung', 26 March.

22 Daily active users in Europe declined by 3 million from 282 million to 279 million in the second quarter, monthly active users in Europe fell by 1 million from 377 million to 376 million. See Facebook's earnings: https://s21.q4cdn.com/399680738/files/doc_financials/201 8/Q2/Q2-2018-Earnings-Presentation.pdf.

23 German Chancellor Angela Merkel initiated the debate after stating at a summit of think tank Global Solutions Initiative in May 2018 that "Pricing data – particularly the data of consumers – is the central issue that we need to solve in order to ensure a fair and equitable world of the future." https://twitter.com/glob_solutions/status/100110989572 1168898. In October 2018, British Chancellor Philip Hammond said the government is considering a new tax for tech companies.

24 Facebook (2018), *Q2 2018 Results*, investor presentation, https://s21.q4cdn.com/399680738/files/doc_financials/201 8/Q2/Q2-2018-Earnings-Presentation.pdf.

25 Haenni, Roger (2017), *Datum White Paper* V15, https://datum.org/assets/Datum-WhitePaper.pdf

26 Eric Posner and Glen Weyl (2018), *Radical Markets. Uprooting capitalism and democracy for a just society.* Princeton University Press.

27 Joe Bish (2015): 'I spent a whole day doing online surveys to see if they can actually make you any money', *Vice*, 24 October.

How do we stay afloat?

1 Watch one of Lachlan's fights on YouTube: www.youtube.com/watch?v=mtc_6sBNxzo.

Job jugglers

1 Willis Towers Watson (2018), The future of work: debunking myths and navigating new realities.
2 See for example: www.carl-jung.net/persona.html.
3 Laura Amazzone (2015), 'Akhilandeshwari: The Power of Brokenness', Sutra Journal, December, www.sutrajournal.com/akhilandeshwari-the-power-of-brokenness-by-laura-amazzone.
4 Iris Bohnet (2016), 'How to take the bias out of interviews', Harvard Business Review, 18 April.
5 Lauren Rivera (2012), 'Hiring as Cultural Matching: The Case of Elite Professional Service Firms', American Sociological Review, Vol 77, Issue 6.
6 Kate Glazebrook (2018), '50,000 applicants have now applied for jobs through Applied!', Medium, 18 October. See also Kate Glazebrook and Janna Ter Meer (2016), 'Can we predict applicant performance without requiring CVs?', Medium, 22 September.
7 Quote taken from Pymetrics' founding story on www.pymetrics.com/about/
8 Edelman Intelligence (2018), Freelancing in America. https://www.slideshare.net/secret/ACjItnwUcPlaOZ.
9 AlphaBeta (2017), The Automation Advantage.
10 Whitney Johnson (2018), 'Why talented people don't use their strengths', Harvard Business Review, 8 May.
11 Upwork (2018), 'What Are the Highest Paid Skills on Upwork? The Top 20 From 2017', blog, 2 February.
12 Peter F. Drucker (2005), 'Managing oneself', Harvard Business Review [reprinted from 1999], http://sbuweb.tcu.edu/jmathis/Org_Mgmt_Materials/Managing_Oneself.pdf.
13 Bond, Suzan (2017), 'Your brain hates self-promotion as much as you do', Fast Company, 18 April.

14 Alan Felstead Alan and Golo Henseke (2017),
    'Assessing the growth of remote working and its
    consequences for effort, well-being and work-life
    balance'. *New technology, work and employment*, 4
    October.
15 International Workplace Group (2018), 'The end of the
    traditional 9-5?', press release, 30 May.

Learning à la carte

1   Duncan McLeod "Shift Happens" (2007)
    http://www.postkiwi.com/2007/did-you-know-shift-
    happens.
2   WEF (2016), *The future of jobs*, chapter 'skills stability',
    http://reports.weforum.org/future-of-jobs-2016/skills-
    stability/#view/fn-15.
3   Ibid.
4   New York Fed (2018), 'Labor Market Outcomes of
    College Graduates by Major', 6 February.
5   TwoPointZero (2017), 'Over half of young Aussies
    regret their electives', press release, 5 September
    www.twopointzero.com.au/insight-post-type/half-young-
    aussies-regret-electives/ TwoPointZero provided us
    with detailed figures for university graduates.
6   OECD (2018), *Education at a Glance 2018*, table A.3.1,
    https://doi.org/10.1787/eag-2018-en.
7   Ibid, indicator A.4.1.
8   University of New England (2017), 'UNE introduces
    bespoke courses', press release, 9 January.
9   EY (2018), Can universities of today lead learning for
    tomorrow? The University of the future, p. 4.
10 OECD (2017), *Education at a Glance 2017*, indicator A5.
11 Ibid.
12 Ed Lee (2018), 'Our best photos deserve to be printed',
    Digital Imaging Reporter's 2018 state of the industry,
    InfoTrends, blog, 12 September. See also: Stephen
    Heyman (2015), 'Photos, photos everywhere', *The New
    York Times*, 29 July.
13 WEF (2016), *The future of jobs*, chapter 'skills stability'.

14 Foundation for Young Australians (2016), *The new work mindset.*

15 Marco Nink (2016), 'The high cost of worker burnout in Germany', *Gallup Business Journal*, 17 March. See also: Gallup (2018), 'Employee Burnout, the five main causes', 12 July.

Building your own armour

1 OECD (2015), *Healthcare costs unsustainable in advanced economies without reform*, www.oecd.org/health/healthcarecostsunsustainableinadv ancedeconomieswithoutreform.htm. Also: OECD (2017), 'Pensions reforms have slowed in OECD countries but need to continue', press release, 5 December. And OECD data on general government debt: https://data.oecd.org/gga/general-government-debt.htm

2 CBS News/AP (2010), Europe Balks at Greece's Retire-at-50 Rules, 17 May.

3 Der Rechnungshof Österreich (2014/15), *Pensionsrecht der Bediensteten der ÖBB*, www.parlament.gv.at/PAKT/VHG/XXV/III/III_00155/imf name_388991.pdf.

4 See for example: www.expatica.com.

5 Quote from Airtasker insurance corporate website: www.airtasker.com/insurance/.

6 See Uber corporate website, *Partner Protection Insurance With AXA*, www.uber.com/en-GB/drive/insurance/

7 Nuremberg Institute for Market Decisions (2016), *Worldwide ranking: trust in professions*, March.

8 Gallup (2018), 'Nurses Again Outpace Other Professions for Honesty, Ethics', 20 December.

9 Brett Arends (2015), "How hedge-fund geniuses got beaten by monkeys — again", *Market Watch*, 25 June.

10 Ibid.

11 Roger Edelen, Richard Evans, and Gregory Kadlec (2016), 'Shedding Light on "Invisible" Costs: Trading Costs and Mutual Fund Performance' *Financial*

Analysts Journal, Vol. 69, issue 1, www.cfapubs.org/doi/abs/10.2469/faj.v69.n1.6. See also Kenneth Kim (2016), 'How Much Do Mutual Funds Really Cost?', *Forbes,* 24 September.

12 BetaShares Exchange Traded Funds, *The Biggest 200, The Smallest Cost,* www.betashares.com.au/a200/ .

13 WealthFront (2018), *How much does Wealthfront charge for its service?,* https://support.wealthfront.com/hc/en-us/articles/211003683-How-much-does-Wealthfront-charge-for-its-service-.

14 Felix Salmon (2018), 'Beware of Roboadvisor bearing low fees', *Wired,* 20 March.

15 Orchard Insurance Services, corporate website: www.orchardinsuranceservices.co.uk/how-to-buy-insurance-using-price-compa.

16 Kara Gammell (2011), 'Car insurance: the pros and cons of using comparison sites', *The Telegraph,* 12 January.

17 See Shlomo Benartzi official website, www.shlomobenartzi.com.

18 Shlomo Benartzi (2017), 'How Digital Tools and Behavioral Economics Will Save Retirement', *Harvard Business Review,* 7 December.

19 Oliver Ralph (2018), 'Identity crisis: the insurers moving away from insurance', *Financial Times,* 6 August.

20 All information from Vitality's corporate website: https://vitality.aia.com.sg.

21 Bruce Japsen (2016), 'UnitedHealth And Qualcomm Launch Wearable Device Coverage Plan', *Forbes,* 1 March.

22 All information from UnitedHealthcare's online advertising material. See for example: www.uhc.com/content/dam/uhcdotcom/en/landing/pdf/UHC-BHCG-Motion-w-HSA-3.pdf.

23 Swiss Re (2016), *Mutual Insurance in the 21st century: back to the Future?*

24 Carolyn Bigda (2015), 'Why renters insurance is worth it', *Chicago Tribune,* 1 September.

25 Insurance Business (2016), 'New P2P insurance system to use bitcoins', 20 May.

My home is my hostel

1 Shelter (2016), 'First time buyers will need £64,000 salary to afford an average home by 2020, warns Shelter', press release, 14 April.

2 Apartment List (2016), American Dream of Homeownership Delayed for Millennial Generation, 16 May.

3 Statistics Netherlands/CBS (2018), 'More Dutch and European young adults living at home', 17 November.

4 See Eurostat data (2017) at https://ec.europa.eu/eurostat/web/products-eurostat-news/-/DDN-20181214-1.

5 Greenpeace (2017), *After the binge, the hangover. Insights into the minds of clothing consumers.*

6 MyHomeMove (2016), 'The secret to Brits falling in love with their home is simple: a perfect location', press release, 29 January.

7 Bank of the West BNP Paribas (2018), *The 2018 Millennial Study: What we found out.*

8 Avital Margalit (2006), 'The Value of Home Ownership', *Theoretical Inquiries in Law 7.2.*

9 Chris Reining (2018), 'Why I'm not rushing to pay off my $100,000 mortgage', *Insider,*12 May.

10 When looking at global housing over a very long time (since 1900), average capital gains shrink to a loss of 2% per year, the study shows. British investors appear slightly better off, with property returns of 1.8% per year over that period. Still, that gain seems paltry compared to overall returns of 5.5% in the British share market in an average year over this period. See: Credit Suisse (2018), *Global Investment Returns Yearbook 2018.*

11 Eurostat (2017), 'People in the EU - statistics on housing conditions'.

12 Jonathan Cribb, Andrew Hood and Jack Hoyle (2018), 'The decline of homeownership among young adults',

Institute for Fiscal Studies, briefing note, 16 February.

13 Apartment List (2018), 2018 Millennial Homeownership Report: American Dream Delayed.

14 Get Living (2018), Millennial living in 2018: insights for the UK build-to-rent sector.

15 Information from Brickx corporate website, www.brickx.com/properties/SLD01/summary.

16 Based on information on the Kohab corporate website: *Co-ownership: what is it, how to do it right,* www.kohab.com/insight/articles/internal/details/co-ownership-what-is-it-how-to-do-it-right.

17 Jake Carter (2018), Millennials unaware of shared ownership, study finds, *Mortgage Strategy*, 10 December.

18 More info on the Atlant website https://atlant.io/.

19 Details taken from the Society One corporate website, www.societyone.com.au/marketplace/rates-and-fees.

20 Information from the Kickstarter campaign website www.kickstarter.com/projects/timbuktu/kickstarter-gold-good-night-stories-for-rebel-girl.

21 Watch Caitlin's campaign video: www.dailymail.co.uk/video/news/video-1192635/Gold-Coast-teen-Caitlin-Argyle-crowd-funds-home.html.

22 Information from Airbnb corporate website: www.airbnb.com.au/help/article/2193/mortgage-refinancing.

23 Fannie Mae (2017), America's Housing Partner. 2017 Progress Report.

24 Jude Landis and Malloy Evans (2018), How Will the Gig Economy Shape Mortgage Lending?, *Fannie Mae Perspectives,* 16 May.

25 As quoted by Benedict Brook (2018), 'A room we take for granted right now will be a thing of the past in future homes, says Ikea', *News.com.au,* 4 June.

26 See Kin – The Co-living Digest website: *The Ultimate List of co-living spaces,* http://getkin.io/coliving-list.

27 See A Landing Pad website: www.alandingpad.com/.

28 Laura Donovan (2015), 'The Netherlands' Brilliant

Solution to Cut College Housing Costs', *Attn:, 6 April.*
29 See La Borda website:
www.laborda.coop/en/project/funding-structure/.
30 Quote taken from interview by Ines Peborde with the
architect in September 2016, as published on La Borda:
www.laborda.coop/wp-content/uploads/2018/12/La-
Borda-Barcelona-New-Europe.pdf.
31 Information from UK Cohousing website:
https://cohousing.org.uk/about/about-cohousing/
32 Peter Jakobsen & Henrik Gutzon Larsen (2018), 'An
alternative for whom? The evolution and socio-
economy of Danish cohousing', *Urban Research &
Practice*, 22 April.
33 TowerGate (2019), Community 2.0: Is CoHousing the
future of Urban Design?

About the authors

Vera Sprothen is a German-Australian journalist and economist with a passion for surfing and untangling the complexities of labour markets. A former reporter with some of the world's largest publications, including *The Wall Street Journal*, *Wirtschaftswoche*, *DIE ZEIT* and *ELLE*, she has written numerous features about the working lives of people around the globe, from Ukrainian day labourers in Germany to vanilla farmers in Tonga. For this book, she recalled her own gig economy experience – as a pizza delivery driver, tobacco vendor and promotion girl – from the days when your mobile phone was still dumb and the internet only a few pages long. Vera holds a Master in Economics and Politics from University of Cologne and is a graduate of Holtzbrinck School for Business Journalists. She is now working in Sydney as a freelance writer, editor and surf instructor helping people find their flow in life.

Nicoló Andreula is an Italian economist, strategist and public speaker. A former management consultant with *McKinsey*, he loves travelling far and wide in the world of work. He has taught maths to slum kids in Kenya, sold prostrate drugs in Japan and honed his financial skills at investment bank *Goldman Sachs* in London. An advisory job in Singapore, where he worked with Google, Uber and Netflix on public policy issues, ignited his fascination with disruptive technology and societal change. This book finally gave him an outlet to draw on his passion for Greek philosophy. Nicoló holds a Master in Economics from Bocconi University and MBA from INSEAD. Based in Puglia, a beautiful Southern Italian region marred by high youth unemployment, Nicoló is working for positive change and living the liquid life himself – as a freelance consultant, corporate trainer and lecturer (Chinese University of Hong Kong).

Made in the USA
San Bernardino,
CA